38

FOTO**TORST**

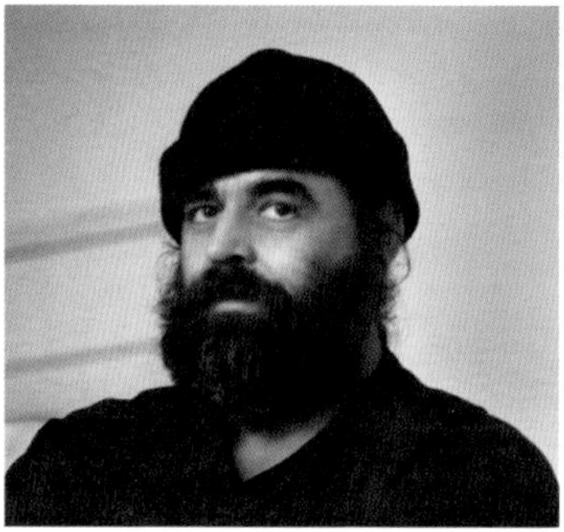

To Walter Nobbe, my dear and inspiring friend
(Malang 1941 – The Hague 2005)

Vojta **Dukát**

TORST

Kniha byla vydána ve spolupráci s Ministerstvem kultury České republiky.

For their kind help, Vojta Dukát thanks Mr Hans Janssen, a curator at the Gemeentemuseum Den Haag, and Mr Miroslav Ambroz, Brno, who designed and edited *A Slice of Time*, the book on which the current publication is based.

Autor děkuje panu Hansi Janssenovi, kurátorovi Gemeente Muzea v Den Haagu, a panu Miroslavu Ambrozovi z Brna za pomoc s přípravou této publikace, která svým obsahem vychází z knihy *A Slice of Time*, jejímž byl editorem a grafikem.

ISBN 978-80-7215-463-0

A Respectful Photographer

The most important thing is knowing what not to photograph
Vojta Dukát

A Moravian photographer, Vojta Dukát has lived in the Netherlands since 1968. There, he has received official recognition for his years of contributing to humanist photography. In 1997, he was awarded the most important Dutch prize for photography, the Capi-Lux Alblas Prijs, and, in 2001, he received the Ouborg Award, a prize for the visual arts, given by the city of The Hague. In connection with the Ouborg Award, a selection of his work came out in a prestigious publication, *A Slice of Time*, intended particularly for a Dutch audience, written in Dutch. In the book, he has successfully mixed reverence with pure, unhackneyed creativity. Though he has admirers in his native land, Dukát has received no awards in the Czech Republic and, till now, no books of his work had ever been published here.

Dukát's photographs do not come out of Moravian or Dutch traditions. Rather, they stem from the European and American traditions of the modern snapshot, the supreme examples of which are the works of the Magnum photographers. As we shall see, however, his works also go a bit beyond that tradition.

Dukát's remaining true to certain values became evident from the moment he entered adult life. He attended a secondary-school for electro-engineering, but did not graduate. (He can, however, repair almost anything.) In the exciting years of the thaw in Czechoslovakia, in 1966–68, still under the Communist régime, he had a number of pleasant jobs. In those days, the supreme goal was freedom. And so, after the occupation of Czechoslovakia by five Warsaw Pact armies in August 1968, Dukát left the country. As his replacement home, he chose the Netherlands, bringing with him an enchantment with cinematography and photography, including "The Family of Man" exhibition, Mario Giacomelli, and some Magnum photographers. It was in Amsterdam, that he found the freedom he needed, studying photography at the Rietveld School of Art & Design, in 1968–70, and cinematography at the Film Academy, in 1970–71. He no longer likes to recall the staged photographs he made of his friends in those days, which conform to the New Wave of film and photography in Czechoslovakia and the hippie movement. One can still see them, for example, in the Bibliothèque nationale,

Paris. Dukát began to wander the world. He learnt new languages easily. He was already recording images that he glimpsed in real life, so well in fact that he was twice nominated for membership in Magnum, in 1974 and 1976. He was ultimately not accepted. (Perhaps he should not have even tried, since he didn't like being told what to do, nor did he want to take photographs of just anything anywhere in the world, rather than simply what he really liked.) Nevertheless, Dukát has fond memories of Magnum. He fell in love with Portugal, where Magnum had sent him in 1975, so much so that he wanted to become Portuguese. But his new homeland, the Netherlands, increasingly came to appreciate Dukát. In 1976, he was granted Dutch citizenship, thus giving him more and more freedom. Among other things, he also continued to take photographs in Portugal. In 1980, an exhibition of his works was held at the Stedelijk Museum Amsterdam, one of the most prestigious art institutions in Europe. What more could one want? But it was just then that Dukát refused to set out on the road that had opened for him.

The problem turned out to be that the more he photographed, the more film he had to deal with. Whereas taking photographs is a free activity, working in the darkroom seemed to Dukát to be too much like the Marxist conception of freedom, the consciousness of necessity. Nevertheless, he tried at least in part to chart out his own life, which resulted, in 1983, in a box (originally for a hundred sheets of 10×15 cm photographic paper) overflowing with prints of his life's work so far. (Unlike, for example, Duchamp's Boîte-en-valise, or box in a suitcase, these prints exist only in one copy each.) When asked, Dukát was happy to show the contents of the box to friends and acquaintances, but he mostly turned a deaf ear to requests to make prints, hold an exhibition, or put together a publication. He continued to make photographs, but they did not end up in little boxes. Some of the film remained undeveloped. He tried to solve the problem, in 1987, by switching to a video camera, but the medium turned out to be even more time consuming. Besides, Dukát did not have, and still does not have, good equipment for editing video cassettes. Instead of rolls of film, he has thus been accumulating piles of cassettes of videos he made in Czechoslovakia, Poland, and Hungary before the Changes of late 1989, and, afterwards, mainly from his former homeland, including Moravian folk customs and music and the withdrawal of Soviet troops, and also in Subcarpathian Ruthenia, which had been part of the first Czechoslovak Republic and remained a land where time seemed to have stood still.

Dukát has devoted a considerable part of his life to collecting old machines, mainly cars, which he doesn't drive. And he makes only the most necessary repairs to the car he drives, so that he can then look forward to something breaking down again. He is thus also an artist of car maintenance. Instead of promoting his photographs, he promotes the Tatra automobile, whose aerodynamic shape was a unique contribution to car design in 1934.

This character sketch was not really necessary as an introduction to Dukát's photographs. It is perhaps only an explanation of why there are so few of them. Nor do his photographs really need explaining. They are inconspicuous black-and-white snapshots; Dukát says that he doesn't see in color. Because they are inconspicuous, it takes a long time to realize how special they actually are. Perhaps they are most different from the usual works of photojournalism; perhaps they are in every respect actually the opposite of photojournalism. With few exceptions, they do not report on actual events, sensation, or celebrities; they have not been taken in a hurry. They are calm, well-balanced, and, if they contain drama, it is somewhere below the surface. This is also what makes them different from the expressive style that was predominant in the 1960s and 1970s, that is, in Dukát's formative years. After photographers like William Klein and Josef Koudelka had taught the viewer, in the interest of the urgency of the message, to accept a provocative photo with things like severely cropped figures, deformations caused by the lens, and printed with high graininess, Dukát returned to an earlier style, long before even this one.

After looking through his photographs for a while, it may seem that Dukát has moved away from the photojournalism paradigms formulated by Robert Capa in the words: "If your photographs aren't good enough, you aren't close enough." A great number of Dukát's photos, perhaps most, are conceived at a respectful distance from the moving parts of the perceived image. Respectful because Dukát respects the perceived images and does not want to violate their authenticity. (When he was growing up, "authenticity" was perhaps the most frequently used word among intellectuals influenced by Existentialism. Back then, however, authenticity was guaranteed by the soul of the artist; for Dukát, authenticity is guaranteed by reality itself.) When, however, he has photographed from up close, it has meant that he was either short of time or of space in which to retreat. Modernists rejected the illusive art of the nineteenth century, which is based on the idealistic notion of the divine wholeness of the world. By contrast, Dukát, consciously or unconsciously, seems to be satisfied with nothing less than a return to an order of some time before the chaos of modern life. That is not so uncommon within the borders of his native land. After all, the great Josef Sudek (1896–1976) did something similar in the field of static photography.

Dukát cuts his photos, like pieces of pie, out of the harmonic whole of the world, whose existence he senses, despite everything. He puts extraordinary emphasis on artistic perfection and also on the naturalness of his compositions. He is a conservative photographer. The impression left by his photographs is often lyrical. The forms in them are usually velvety, wrapped in the light that organizes the world.

What kind of world is that? It is indisputably the contemporary world; there is no alternative for photography. But it is not the contemporary world of rushing around, producing, and consuming. After a moment of looking at a Dukát photo, the viewer begins to realize that Dukát's world lacks contemporary architecture, banks, modern transport, and almost everything that characterizes the present day. By contrast, these photographs contain much of the past that is embedded in the present, the old way of life and old sense of life, both now vanishing. Some of the photos from small towns and villages contain things that really can be confusing. For example, in the south there are timeless clothes (a skirt or trousers, a white blouse or a shirt) and timeless activities (like hanging out the washing). Consequently, it is quite easy to mistake a work by Dukát with a photo that is a hundred years old. Something similar is also true of the photos of folk customs and festivals. Documentary photographers have always tried to conserve what the march of civilization has passed the death sentence on. Dukát's works, moreover, contain a respect for the previous history of his medium, which he does not try to surmount with revolutionarily new works. On the contrary, he aims to lag behind as much as possible so that he can respectfully look at the classics from the back, and take photographs that would probably not have been new in the past, but are today.

Most of Dukát's photographs show nothing exotic. They are photos of the most everyday aspects of everyday life, wholly in the spirit of the predominant art tradition of the former Czechoslovakia. What is unusual, however, is what the photographer has selected from everyday life. He himself talks about taking photographs of solitude. But that is not precise. The lonely people in

Dukát's photographs always go beyond themselves, because the photographer has put them into relations with other things and other people, into a larger whole that they do not see because they cannot get out of their own skins in order to look at themselves. They usually don't notice how the photographer sees them, but perhaps later they always identify with his pictures, and we do too. After all, who wants to be alone? Who doesn't want to be part of a higher harmony? Dukát brings to mind the venerable role of works of art as messengers of consolation and a desire to make the world a better place.

Antonín Dufek, 2001, 2013

The Osip Mandelstam of Photography *

Sometimes there lies on the shores of an unruffled sea, at the foot of an uninhabited mountain range or amidst sun-baked lowlands where one would hardly expect a hamlet or a solitary house, a town.

This sentence, with the grammatical subject at the very end (like a car with its engine above the rear axle), is the opening of the 1937 novel *De Opstand van Guadálajara* (The Guadalajara Uprising), by the Dutch author Jan Slauerhoff.

I have always considered it one of the most beautiful introductory sentences in our literature, and even had it not served as an introductory sentence it would still be a breathtaking formula.

From time to time this sentence comes to my mind, usually spontaneously, and sporadically during my travels, when I happen upon places where one might possibly settle for just an imaginary town.

And in rare, unique cases, it appears that these kinds of towns actually exist.

I was once in Novgorod, Russia, and for miles around there was nothing to indicate that one was on the way to Novgorod. But the same might happen to you also in Italy, where certain towns lie not at the foot, but right at the top, of a barren mountain range: Cortona, Urbino, Perugia.

And there is also a fourth occasion that brings Slauerhoff's sentence to mind: that is, while observing some of Vojta Dukát's photographs. If I paraphrase it carefully, I arrive at approximately this formulation: sometimes there arises, at the edge of a completely deserted square, on the bank of an otherwise inconspicuous canal or in a place where one would hardly expect the presence of a person, a photograph. Emphasis is on the first specification, sometimes, since, on closer inspection, these images could only have been made by Vojta Dukát.

Through what is mentioned above I have directly touched on what is, in my opinion, a unique quality of Dukát's work: the fact that it shows no similarities to that of another photographer, and vice versa, I cannot recollect any photographer whose shots would resemble Dukát's photographs. At the most, Dukát's work comes close to photographs that you could imagine, were you to possess sufficient imagination, or photographs you want to create yourself, if you are vain enough. Dukát is a complete original, and only outside photography can I recollect the names of a few artists whose position could be described in a similar manner.

It may be significant that poetry, in particular, comes to mind (at least to mine): Emily Dickinson's poems resemble only other poems by Emily Dickinson. Osip Mandelstam does not resemble anyone else; the only success his imitators ever achieved was in demonstrating that he cannot be imitated. But one does not have to go that far. The poetry of Elisabeth Eybers, written in Afrikaans, defies any attempt at association with other poetry: "Wanneer die erts geskei is van die steen / moet dit gesmelt, ontsmet word en gesmee / voor dit in suiwerheid te-voorskyn tree." (Once the ore is separated from the stone / it needs to be smelted, purged and forged / before it emerges in its purity.)

Suiwerheid, purity is, in my opinion, another quality of Dukát's. However, I admit that this term is often misused, and few assessments are as dubious as those based on the adjective "authentic." The world is full of things that are authentic and at the same time totally inane. To explain more clearly what I mean by "purity" in the photography of Vojta Dukát, I must first tell a story.

One January, when I was in St. Petersburg (for reasons that are not important here), it was snowing, freezing, perhaps twelve degrees below zero, and I was cold. I decided to do something I had always avoided during my previous visits to Russia: to buy *a shapka* (a fur cap). I asked a Russian who had become attached to our group where it would be best to get one, and he referred me to a department store on Nevsky Prospekt, by the Anichkov Bridge. The details are not relevant; it is the scene that met my eyes as I stepped over the threshold that matters. First the floor – just like the floors in every shop in St. Petersburg in January – was covered in a foul layer of muddy, half-melted snow; I realized, the second I passed the door, that I hadn't given the tiniest thought to this in all the time I'd been out of Russia. And then the interior itself: a hulk of a space, all the plaster filthy, bulging and cracking, the swinging doors dangling from worn-out hinges, and something resembling a counter in a variation of dark-brown wood from which, as if from a ship's bow, an old woman glared at the rabble shopping below. At the same time, this whole symphony of absurd detail, the pathetic specifics of which I have forgotten, reminded me (more insistently than my plane landing) that I was in Russia. I did buy my *shapka*. For three hundred thousand rubles.

Some two months later, Hripsimé Visser showed me, in the Stedelijk Museum Amsterdam, a selection she had made of Vojta Dukát's photographs. Like everyone else, I knew his work only superficially. It has seldom been exhibited or published. One of the first examples I saw came into existence in 1985, in what was then Leningrad. One can see a clock which from the moment the photograph was taken shows a quarter to one, and a counter, and behind it such a Russian *dyezhurnaya* (supervisor), keeping a sharp eye on the scene. A glimpse of the street behind the glass swinging door is vaguely visible. Two women are at the door, one of them entering, the other leaving. Nothing more than a few loose, coincidental facts, but it was like when you hear the opening bars of a symphony that you haven't heard for ages. These first bars were enough to fill a gap in the musical memory, not in real time but literally in a flash: this was the building where I had been two months earlier in a different year, under different circumstances, but with the same smell, the same fluid chiaroscuro, the same electrifying impact on the perception. In other words: the same feeling of authenticity.

This, however, is a rather simple example and it is entirely thanks to coincidence that a personal experience should provide the means to verify it. It becomes far more complicated with those of Dukát's images that are, so to speak, delivered by a second hand, or with those that have completely broken away from their natural environment. One particularly extreme example is a Dukát photograph taken in 1979 in Zurich, of a woman and a man sitting down for a smoke in a cafe. The strange thing is – or at least I find it strange – that the man has varnished fingernails. They are clearly recognizable as darkish points; they even possess their own individual shine. Everything else seems to be blurred – the room itself, the expression on the woman's face, the way in which she is sitting, and, in the final reckoning, even the meaning that may be attached to the image. And yet it is no less authentic than the photograph of a St. Petersburg interior.

But what about the meaning? We now come up against a reflex that is both incorrigible and enigmatic, in which we want to ascribe a meaning to photographs, no matter how unsharp, how mundane, or how cursory they might be. It is almost a compulsive task: someone has put the effort into registering a certain situation, and this itself generates a premise, an ontological imperative, that has to lead to more or less concrete implications: what is expressed, what is concealed behind it, why was the photograph taken – these kinds of questions. Every photograph pushes one into writing a caption for it. It is interesting in this context that, as surveys have shown, newspaper readers devote more time letting the caption under a photograph penetrate their minds than to the "reading" of the photograph itself. Such is the practice also at exhibitions in museums ... there is an A4 sheet with captions or rather with names of places where each photograph was taken.

In a church-like space, a woman can be seen dressed in some kind of floral-pattern pajamas. Next to her, at a small table with a lace cover, sits a man, looking on seriously. A man is sitting next to him, in a black jacket. He has something like a horse blanket on his lap. Below, a mere glimpse of his bare feet.

A man is walking across the picture. Under his arm, he is carrying a heavy object that looks like a door. In the foreground a girl in a dress that is slightly too large for her, stands with her arm around the shoulders of an old woman. They both are looking into the lens, the old lady in a somewhat misty way.

A man is hunched over a table, sleeping. On the table is a teacup, a glass, and an ashtray. In the background, a passer-by is peeping inside through a steamed-up window. He has dark glasses, his face resembling that of Primo Levi.

In a room with a checkered carpet stand a man and a woman. It is not quite clear whether they are dancing or whether the woman is just about to slap the man. In the background, under a monumental staircase, a solitary woman in long trousers practices dance steps.

Four photographs. The captions: *Western Samoa* 1973, *Oporto* 1979, *Zurich* 1979, *Blackpool* 1978. It is remarkable that the texts are, even regardless of their uniform style, nearly completely interchangeable. The Zurich photograph could well have been taken – it seems – in Blackpool and the 1973 photograph in the year 1979. In part, the reason is that Dukát's work is almost completely timeless (in the sense that his photographs do not contain any references to their times of origin). Another reason is that Dukát takes photographs of situations that lack all too specific hallmarks, a revealing anecdote or a too obvious commitment.

Where specificity is lacking, its place is often taken by symbolism. This approach is widely employed in all attempts to make photography, in artistic terms, *salonfähig* – "presentable in 'higher' society" – from Alfred Stieglitz to André Kertész, from Albert Renger-Patzsch to Nobuyoshi Araki. I think we would be going too far if, in Dukát's case, we were to talk in terms of symbolic or symbolist photographs. A symbol always entails a hidden agreement concerning the relationship between a sign and what it symbolizes. To prevent too much confusion, a certain system is essential. And there is, naturally, the interpretation – so at least the symbol can be successfully decoded.

My impression is that Dukát has taken a completely different path, and that the best way to shed light on the meaning of his photographs lies in what I, in a nutshell, would call the "image-as-such." I admit that it is a far from perfect term, but for the time being I do not have any better. To clarify it, allow me a short diversion into the history of literature.

At the beginning of the twentieth century, a current flowed through Russian poetry, known rather problematically as Acmeism. It comes from the Greek *acme*, meaning a peak or the highest point – a mountain top. Acmeists, the most important of whom included Anna Akhmatova, Nikolay Gumilev, and Osip Mandelstam, shared the opinion that, with their predecessors the symbolists, the language had arrived, by the fact that every word could acquire an arbitrary number of new, symbolic meanings, at such a point of confusion that it was necessary to renew the correspondence between the word and the object. The language had to be, as it were, purified of all lexical vagaries and mysticism, of all verbal inflation. Words had to be placed once more at the height of their original meanings, in their primary shapes, to be sharpened and written down. It is the word-as-such, in Russian *slovo kak takovoye*. And this primary form refers, above all, to a concrete, pure, or, if you like, mundane reality. In one of their manifestos, the Acmeists formulated it thus:

> The struggle between Acmeism and Symbolism is, above all, a struggle for this world, for its sounds, its colors, its shapes, its weight and time; it is a struggle for our planet Earth. For Acmeists, a rose is once again beautiful for what it is, for its blossoms, for its smell and its color, not for an imaginary affinity with mystical love, or anything else.

Two examples highlight the simplicity the Acmeists pursued. Akhmatova wrote a poem in which, describing her nervousness, she says that she is trying to stick her right hand in a left glove. Mandelstam is the author of a poem in which the following lines appear: "We sit in the kitchen, you and I, / Sweet smells the white kerosene. There is no need for a further description of the nervousness. Glove and kerosene, 'the word-as-such', are fuel enough."

The tale of photography includes an endless tally of statements by photographers who have felt obliged to overhaul the truth through this medium. "Photography is my passion, searching for truth is my obsession," wrote the

American photographer Alfred Stieglitz. There is nothing special about this; some say that every direction taken by art, every ism, however abstract or abstruse, is inclined to attach the label of realism to itself. But it hardly renders the use of a language any plainer. Twenty years ago, Michael Dummett, an important English philosopher, wrote a book with the remarkable title *Truth and Other Enigmas* (1978). If only for this fact, it is well and good that from time to time appear artists, poets, and photographers who at least give the impression that they want to start again from scratch; from a word or an image in its purest and most ingenuous form; in other words, from the image-as-such.

The long shadow of Romanticism sees to it that even the simplest notions can hardly be understood without the person who perceives them feeling in some way emotionally moved by them. Moreover, it often appears that there exists something like an active willingness to be moved in this way. Everyone knows the feeling generated by archaeological finds, especially if the objects are associated with everyday reality: mosaics in Roman baths, a dress buckle, a random inscription – "Thou, silent form, dost tease us out of thought / As doth Eternity". This is the pre-eminently Romantic equation called up by Keats in his celebrated "Ode on a Grecian Urn": "Beauty is truth, truth beauty." And this is the selfsame match that, nearly two hundred years later, is still solemnized in many a mind. It even reaches the extent that objects that have not directly been excavated but are in some way archaic or exotic, and at the same time ordinary, mine a Romantic vein. I would call this the "tourist variation": to go to an obscure place at the edge of a well-known continent, to Portugal, Istanbul, a Moscow suburb, the north of Scotland, and in any of them find a fisherman, someone shining shoes, a tiny workshop or a ruin, a theme that can make the ordinary look like something apparently extraordinary. To take a photograph, just press the button. And even this effort is not always needed. In Tuscany, you can buy posters assembled from perhaps a hundred small photographs of front doors, the proverbial picturesque quality of which can fully meet the demands of any Romantic fondness for cliché. Lost in their dreams, vacationers purchasing the posters are probably not in the least aware that they are not taking home a true picture but merely an accepted symbol of Tuscany.

Indeed, Dukát has not sought out the easiest of twilight areas in which to work. He has truly managed to heave overboard the ballast carried for more than a century in the history of photography. He understands that specificity is often disguised as a symbol. Ignoring the confusion of the times, he has again set out in quest of the inherent poetry of the photographic image.

A girl stands under an orange tree. Or at least one thinks it is an orange tree. She appears to be looking into the camera lens. On the left, in a doorway, an elderly man stands leaning against the doorframe. He is smoking a cigarette. The number of the house, 6, appears over the door. In 600 years, the girl will still be looking into the lens, just as that clock in St. Petersburg will always show a quarter to one.

In Bolivia, a woman stands in a billiard hall. She is alone. She is holding a cue, and her position is almost perfectly symmetrical. Through two doors, a view of the street opens up. Two more doors and a gutter are visible. Another cue and a white ball lie on the billiard table.

In Cracow, a cast-iron street lamp stands in the foreground of a deserted factory complex. A young boy is walking by, not aware of anything yet. He is trying to keep a football in the air.

In Burgos, Spain, two blind women in winter coats are walking along the street. They both have walking sticks, and one has a tape recorder on a strap around her neck. Only God knows what is going on inside them, but in any case they give the impression that they have decided to have a cheerful kind of day.

Four women of an uncertain age stand under an oval picture of the Virgin Mary. Poland 1982. It must be shortly after Wojciech Jaruzelski declared martial law. They are waiting, but one cannot see what for. One of them has lifted her left foot, leaning it, or perhaps rubbing it, against her right shin.

What does this express? What does such a photograph mean? And is this still a question?

In a commentary written for an exhibition in Prague, in 1995, Vojta Dukát says:

> It is good and very exciting to take the liberty, with humility however, of observing and approaching images at the moment of their genesis, to try at least a few times during one's lifetime to capture those seemingly perfect ones, those we want to see, those we in fact already know and which to an increasingly lesser degree still occasionally do surface from everyday situations.

It is expressed subtly, almost incidentally: "those we in fact already know."

It is a higher form of symbolism in which someone, thanks to their ability to see in an exceptional manner, is able to recover meaning from reality.

It is the memory of what there was no need to agree upon.

Melchior de Wolff

* Originally a speech given by Melchior de Wolff at the Stedelijk Museum Amsterdam during the presentation of the Capi-Lux Alblas Prize to Vojta Dukát in 1997, for his long-standing contribution to visual communication.

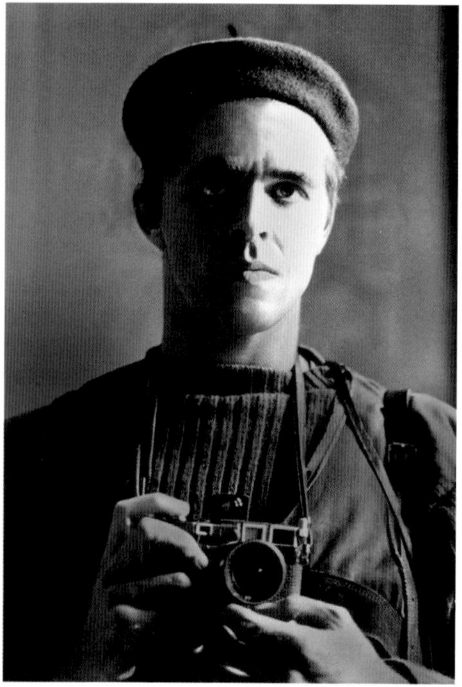

Vojta Dukát, self-portrait / autoportrét, 1977

Two essays by Vojta Dukát

It is good and very exciting to take the liberty, with humility however, of observing and approaching images at the moment of their genesis, to try and at least a few times during one's lifetime to capture those seemingly perfect ones, those we want to see, those we in fact already know and which occasionally, but to an increasingly lesser degree, do surface from everyday situations. To behold, if only for a moment, even the less than perfect ones can be enriching, just as we draw from images that have been encountered and rescued by others, providing we have been allowed to peer into them. They then live on with us, can become our nourishment, we can rely on them, commune with them, they heal and never disappoint.

I hope that this origination against their will, the fact that they often signify what they did not intend to, or all that their advent illuminates in the intricate labyrinths of our hearts does not pain them. I also often recollect the moments which have escaped, where everything did not stop all at once, something, just some tiny something was missing and they did not turn into images, they could not come into being...[1]

It is from these situations:

"When everything suddenly falls silent for a moment,
as in places where birds do not sing,
where something here or somewhere around us,
yet still quivers, ever so slightly trembling..."[2]

that images emerge, where time has momentum, and which will sparkle long after they have ceased to exist. Tell me, how long the train's been gone? Was it really, really nice? Does beauty rest in the eyes of the beholder? Is truth, if it exists, as intricate and hidden as a crown of feathers? Similar questions were once posed by pensive mortals, searching for the debris of images of their era a long time ago when the classics were still alive. Fortunately, they were not born later, otherwise they would have left us neither the means to examine our conscience nor spells of eternal beauty and power.

Looking is not always free from injury. Do we continually need new images if they are not better than those we have already set our eyes on in the past and have possessed for a long time? Are we able to dispose in time of those that our instinct has rejected, if we sense they do not belong to us? It is ever more difficult to go on looking without being reminded of something. Unfortunately, more often than not, of something better. I have an exercise: in the beginning there was the Word; it seemed enough then: [3]

It was late evening, the first of May – a May evening – it was the time of love ... (but look past the iambus – a little further to the lake) – where the voice of the turtledove called to love – where the scent of the pine grove was fragrant...[4]

and now, one of ours:

Once there were times, yes there were
but they have passed away,
and, a little while we also may
and when we have passed the landscape will as well,
as if the top of the rosemary had fallen away...[5]

and one more:

A tree is bouncing against another one
a bird flies in between...from other one to one,
not unlike our love seems to be...[5]

What we have just seen is the garden of paradise and this view may only ever be surpassed by entering the garden itself...This is what we should clean our minds with every day. We should not lend these images to anyone. Especially not the oldest, they may vanish, become irretrievable, never to return. We would then become empty vessels and the multimedia would slurp us up in an instant...And to see, from then on only the emperor's new clothes?...then, Mr. Gottlieb nothing would help us anymore, no holy water, not even the *shem*...[6]...there would be no one to be helped...Mr. Gottlieb, don't jump out of the window, you live on the ground floor! Rilke made similar observations already and as you know: there have only been two wars since, then the communists, then the former ones, then *bolševník*,[7] clothes with inscriptions on them, baseball caps, and now multi-media – but there was and always will be the sparkle in the eyes of the beloved... let's wait a little and, before it all passes away, you can join me:

> ...let God be praised that I was born,
> that I could enjoy the days of my youth,
> those were the only ones I had in this world,
> now they are gone, there are no others to be had.
> O man, beware, you are nothing but ashes and mud,
> when you come to be judged by the Lord of lords
> no excuse will help you...[5]

Vojta Dukát, 1995

Notes

1 Excerpt from "Images and Words" by T. S. Gottlieb, a collection of texts based on interviews with V. Dukat, to be published by Lucid, Brno, Moravia.
2 Excerpts from the poem "Dancing Rays" by T. S. Gottlieb, from the collection *Quiet Friendships*, New York: Mark Kalisch, 1974.
3 Fragments of correspondence between V. Dukát and T. S. Gottlieb.
4 Excerpt from the poem *Máj* (1836), by K. H. Mácha.
5 Excerpts from Moravian folk songs.
6 The magic substance which can resuscitate the Golem.
7 Hogweed.

Texts 1–5 were translated by V. Dukát, The Hague, in collaboration with J. E. Keats (Cambridge, UK).

The most important thing is to know "what not to photograph"[1] if, whatever it is, that will later remain on paper – regardless of all that it could have meant before it got there – will not become something rather flat, bordered off, trying to separate itself by its edges from the space where it is now against its will, where it does not belong..., will not render something which still shows an interest in us,... and is therefore still worth being repaid at least by a quick glance ... which will instantly – allow us to sense the real, more dense and complex image beyond ...

Which is not that thing you are looking at – that paper is just a photograph!

I mean: "just being drawn toward it! – not grabbing or G-d forbid analyzing and verbalizing – what in fact is not there. The only acceptable way to comment on images is Silence... or at the most – an inarticulate murmur, an echo of sorts... resounding a strictly private stream of consciousness at times producing an involuntary sigh: Aaah... which, if it could be translated, would in philosophical terms even surpass the value of an in itself already a very exciting, at the first glance seemingly logical, realization:

Again and again, the sea always seems so vast, serene and so endlessly infinite – almost like, ... like ... like a sea ...[2]

A mighty experience, which nowadays one would most likely and most unfortunately not be too eager to share too often with others in public or dare to try to publish in prestigious international art magazines under his name – without being suicide prone, that is... We all know the essence of the murmur about the sea very well, being nothing new, yet becoming better and better each time – might it be on various occasions and for different reasons – we again and again do come to the same conclusion: then a "New" more profound and experienced "Old" comes to life. That is the "New" which, if shared with others on a wider scale, could be the badly needed soothing and healing contribution to mankind and a certain compensation for the pain caused by the results of the contrived brain activities "of another order" – the results of which most museums of contemporary art and the art magazines which consort with them usually bring us today. It could have that appeasing and quieting effect, the one that one is often besieged by while looking at a sea – so endlessly infinite, vast, eternal as all that – what in fact is not there – fused together – as that which one might have once sensed beyond some flat and square surfaces – and which, again and again, evoked that feeling of tranquility and serenity, one willingly succumbs to – as they are often as familiar to us as those we sense while looking at a sea, which Again and again seems so...

It is, and not only according to me, most unfortunate, that these sensations are far too often not triggered by something that is created under the artificial pressure of "innovation at all costs", instigated, so it seems, by those curators eagerly yearning for new discoveries, enhanced by, in this respect a dangerously high speed of exchange of information and even by the mere existence of time zones. Somewhere, it's today... somewhere else it already means yesterday and then... it could already be too late in order to be The Very First... and the whole world would implode...

That – what usually likes to be later described as provocatively progressive – is often only showy daringness, remains mostly intentionally fragmentary, pretending once again to unravel the mystery of yet another Taboo ... and definitely a "big and ambitious something". That – what is usually hard to get – not only through the many undersized museum doors, built without sufficient foresight in a bygone era, no longer suited to the needs of a contemporary artist... but most importantly, later on – without pain and intimidation – even more difficult to squeeze into the more mature, visually sophisticated and more discriminating minds – which, if at all, then only sporadically yearn for what already long ago became widely known as the everyday, run-of-the-mill, visually incompetent, conceptual photo-monumentalism.

However: in the meantime, go on looking at what there "is" around you, but "see" and hope to get only what will remain – when "is" turns into "was" and becomes just a preferably not too large, flat and oblong ... for ever, but where on its surface "even a little bit will become more" and can – if it is able to put itself in a reverse mode – again reach, preferably even surpass, the original dimensions of what you intended – and I hope in the first place for us – would remain in the end...

That, what is not..., but is so often the subject of interest of many..., can be visualized only by what is... Then – what is can withdraw and make space for what is not... In this way more can become less or even nothing – if that has been your intention... without the need to make the attempt to visualize the invisible... in the end "invisible" again. Be it by the omnipresent nagging ego of the artist – permanently blocking the view – or by surrounding and covering it with a wobbly questionable verbal scaffolding by which it would have to be permanently supported… written and willingly supplied by those who, just like the scaffolding, become an integral, at times even the most dominant, element of the artistic attempts that had to be rescued in this way… while, in doing so, the often very ambitious Verbal causes further pollution of the already heavily infested domain of the Visual.

In case that, be it just a tiny fragment of "that" which surrounded you "then", is still worth even just a fleeting glance… then it can, according to our own needs, depending on the level of the "by you – in us" initiated momentary state of excitement and arousal of our senses, reach even such monumental proportions – you could not have even dreamt about … but, measurable solely in units of Aaah …, the so-far not standardized floating variable of the intensity of visual experiences intricately tied only to our own needs at that point in time …

Monumental proportions?

Yes, but in a more modest sense of the word… whereby the "monumentality" of the "inner images" created by us would reach only such proportions which we still dare to be confronted with… only as large, that the density of a visual experiences would remain a sensible enriching contribution in relation to the cm^4 of that occasionally even four-dimensional imaginary space, where the mysterious "Je ne sais quoi"[3] had chosen to reside…

The minimal requirements being: Aaah… on N/ imaginary $cm^2 > cm^2$ of the carrier.[4]

If you, until now, did not at least once wake up from a dream in a sweat, were in a flash – something appeared that you in fact knew without ever seeing it in the flesh – till now – not knowing you were in fact in waiting – but the Ruler of dreams who allowed you that glance, decided not to provide you with that Finger to press the shutter yet – and it was gone, gone forever and from now on, you will have to live with that gone image all by yourself, forever and forever and forever till the end of time…making you realize, that you don't know what you got until you loose it, but must get it first…

Don't buy a camera!

You will see nothing more – than only what there "is" – through it anyway… It's that simple and it can save you a lot of money… and in case mere unchannelled ambitions proved, after all, to be the true reason to have to change your pajamas in the night… it is the best guarantee that sometime in the future my eye will not stumble over your very big-big and very contemplative visual nothings with a A4 next to them explaining all you have so skillfully concealed from me – except: Why? – since: the Why not – became the answer. The true reason for their existence – that even the objects of no substance must contain – will never reveal itself, it is meant never to be understood unless we really want to tamper with their integrity in a larger context one day… Those who still raise the question – Why do I have to look at it? – will get an instant replay by watching the shadows of your Guardian Angel whose stable you will have to belong to – dancing around it in the limelights, visualizing the true message… reminding you of the rules of the parasitic symbioses of KIN,[5] and us, of the not very immaculate conception of these impious alliances, the fruits of which are so often displayed to innocent souls who still have not – "forever abandoned hope" – entering the contemporary "Cathedrals of What is Not."

Do not despair… the road to salvation is still open…

Go… while there is still time… and learn to make… let's see… say – a good soup!… perhaps the one made from sour milk, fresh dill, caraway seed, potatoes, salt, a touch of vinegar, a little bit of flour, a bit of sugar perhaps and a hard-boiled egg – the one with the nice yellow yolk.[6] It's beautiful to see, good, warm, and it has great nutritional value, so most importantly – don't gobble all of the medicine yourself – think of the neediest first – so, please do give your Guardian Angel the bigger half and the recipe as well.

By this deed FAME will find you instantly and you will be remembered by mankind forever… till the end of time.

I promise! Good night.

Vojta Dukát, 2002, 2012

Notes

1 Excerpts from notes by Vojta Dukát on "Professional intellectualization and glorification of incompetence", the chapter "What not to feed to your Guardian Angel", Copyright V. Dukát 2002. Originally written in 2002 as an additional comment on the text "The most important thing is to know what not to photograph," written by A. Dufek, PhDr., about V. Dukát, in 2001. Excerpts from interviews by Aleš Vašíček with Vojta Dukát were added in 2012. Aleš Vašíček, "The role of a curator in the exhibition-making process", M.A. Visual Thesis; teacher: Bas Vroege; supervisor: Professor Susan Meiselas, University of Leiden, the Netherlands, 2010.

2 A text accompanying a cartoon most likely depicting a "young female servant looking at the sea". (Dukát's own interpretation of the original image does not necessarily match what the artist might have had in mind while making the drawing.) The text used in this essay in connection with the cartoon is Dukát's free interpretation of the original version of the text which he can no longer exactly recall. Dukát only remembers the strong effect it had on him then and still has now. Published in *Literární noviny* (ČSSR), +/- 1968.

3 "Je ne sais quoi" – "a certain something of intangible quality."

4 Aaah on N/ imaginary cm^2 > cm^2 of the carrier, © Vojta Dukát, 2012.

5 KIN, Kunst Industrie Normen, EU – Art Industry Norms, EU; AIN, Art Industry Norms, USA, © V. Dukát 2001.

6 The art of cooking: a very simple recipe for a very beautiful, good, and nutritious dill soup, according to the recipe of the author's grandmother, Mrs. Jenovéfa Volánková of Brno, Moravia.

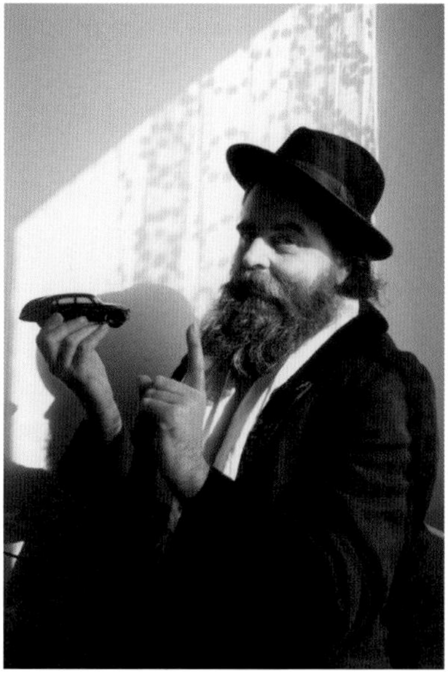

Tatra Art
productions

Brno-The Hague-Paris-New York

The Tatra according to Dukát *

The collaboration, inventiveness, and craftsmanship of the people of different ethnic backgrounds who participated in the synthesis of elegance and exciting and resourceful engineering in the former Czecho-Slovakia, with its epicenter in Moravia, the most industrious part of the former Austro-Hungarian Empire, was a unique and to this day unmatched contribution to automobile design. It produced a unique and extremely noble object "of awesome unearthly beauty of the highest order and gravity-defying density" by which it was levitated and propelled forward – unaffected by the ubiquitous natural elements and physical laws. The Tatra 77 sublimated from an ordinary automobile made of matter into a symbol of "everything good that has yet to come" from the moment its three headlights, beaming photons beyond infinity through the gloomy darkness of the remains of the postwar economic crisis, illuminated that vast space ahead which back then was still called the Future. The descent of the Tatra 77 to Earth in 1934 caused the still quite incomprehensible slowing down of the expansion of the universe and an instantaneous compression of all values known to man at that point in time – thus forcing the third millennium to arrive in pre-war Czecho-Slovakia 67 years ahead of the rest of the world. The 1933 Tatra prototype, the Tatra V570, was copied as the KdF in the Third Reich, and became the famous VW Beetle in postwar Germany. Nor can one resist the feeling that the Tatra 77 line was later inconspicuously reflected in, and superbly refined by, Citroën's ID/DS series in the Sixties – being somewhat of a Tatroid or a Tatroën, if you like – at least according to some fervent Tatra fundamentalists. After the collapse of the Austro-Hungarian Empire (the First EU, as it is sometimes called) in 1918, Moravia was represented on the international stage only by the dash between Czecho-Slovakia and by the silence between the two national anthems. The break-up of the Czech and Slovak Federative Republic in 1993 produced a new, Czech-only republic; and a new, permanent silence after the equally Czech-only national anthem gained new information value and is becoming increasingly more challenging.

* Excerpt from the short essay "The Tatra Millennium". The original version was written as a comment to "The Most Important Thing Is to Know What Not to Photograph," by Antonín Dufek, PhDr., about Vojta Dukát in 2002. Further notes added in 2013.

Uctivý fotograf

„Nejdůležitější je vědět, co nefotit."
Vojta Dukát

Moravský fotograf Vojta Dukát žije od roku 1968 v Nizozemí. Zde byl oficiálně oceněn jeho dlouhodobý přínos humanistické fotografii. Dukát byl roku 1997 odměněn nejdůležitější nizozemskou cenou pro fotografy Capi-Lux Alblas Prijs a kulturní cenou města Den Haag za rok 2001. V souvislosti s cenou města Den Haag byl publikován prestižní výběr Dukátova díla *A Slice of Time*, určený zejména jeho spoluobčanům v Nizozemí, s texty v holandštině. V knize se úspěšně mísí pieta s ryzí a neotřelou tvořivostí. V rodné zemi má Vojta Dukát obdivovatele, ale Česká republika neoplývá cenami ani publikačními možnostmi.

Dukátovy fotografie nevyrůstají z moravské nebo nizozemské tradice, nýbrž z euroamerické tradice moderní momentní fotografie, reprezentované na nejvyšší úrovni agenturou Magnum. Ale jak uvidíme, jsou to díla posunutá o kousek jinam.

Lpění na určitých hodnotách se u Vojty Dukáta projevilo v obvyklé době „vstupu do života". Nedokončil elektroprůmyslovou školu (ale umí skoro všechno spravit) a ve vzrušených letech tání komunistického režimu 1966–68 střídal řadu příjemných zaměstnání. Hodnotou na první příčce pomyslné stupnice pro něho byla svoboda, a tak po okupaci Československa vojsky Varšavské smlouvy v roce 1968 emigroval. Za náhradní domov si vybral Nizozemí. Ze starého domova si přinesl okouzlení filmem a fotografií (výstavou *Family of Man*, Mariem Giacomellim, některými fotografy Magna). Potřebnou míru svobody našel v Amsterdamu na Rietveld Akademie, kde studoval fotografii (1968–70), a na Film akademie, kde k fotografické kameře přidal i filmovou (1970–71). K inscenovaným fotografiím přátel z té doby, poplatným nové vlně filmu a fotografie v Československu i hnutí hippies, se dnes nehlásí, ale je možno je vidět například v pařížské Bibliothèque nationale. Začal se toulat po světě, snadno se učil jazyky. To už fotografoval „zahlédnuté obrazy", dost dobré na to, aby byl dvakrát nominován do Magna (1974, 1976). Nebyl přijat, snad to ani neměl zkoušet. Neuměl ani poslouchat, ani nechtěl fotografovat kdekoli na světě a ihned všechno, nejen to, co by rád. Dukát ale na Magnum vzpomíná v dobrém, zamiloval si alespoň Portugalsko, kam ho Magnum v roce 1975 vyslalo, a to natolik, že se chtěl stát Portugalcem. Nový domov v Nizozemí si však Vojty Dukáta stále víc vážil, roku 1976 ho přijal jako svého občana a umožňoval mu stále svobodnější život, mimo jiné i dále fotografovat v Portugalsku. V roce 1980 se uskutečnila jeho výstava ve Stedelijk muzeu v Amsterdamu, jedné z nejprestižnějších uměleckých institucí v Evropě. Co víc si přát? Byl to však snad přesně tento okamžik, kdy fotograf odmítl nastoupit cestu, která se před ním otevřela.

Problémem se ukázala být nezměnitelná zákonitost přibývání kinofilmů, které by měly být nějak zpracovány. Fotografování je celkem svobodnou činností, kdežto pobyt v černé komoře se příliš blíží marxistickému pojetí svobody jako poznané nutnosti. Přesto se Vojta Dukát pokusil alespoň částečně zmapovat sebe sama a tato jeho snaha vyústila po roce 1983 do jedné přeplněné krabičky na stovku fotopapírů 10×15 cm, naplněné pozitivy reprezentujícími autorovo životní dílo. (Na rozdíl například od kufříků s dílem Marcela Duchampa existují jen v jednom exempláři.) Krabičku její majitel rád na požádání ukazoval přátelům a známým, ale k žádostem o zhotovení zvětšenin, o výstavy a o publikace zůstával většinou hluchý. Dílo pokračovalo, v krabičkách však nepřibývalo, mnohé filmy zůstaly nevyvolané. Problém se měl vyřešit přechodem na filmování videokamerou (1987), ale video se ukázalo být ještě větším požíračem času a na zpracování videokazet nemá Dukát dodnes dobré zařízení. Namísto filmů se tedy vrší videokazety, z Československa, Polska a Maďarska před rokem 1989 a nyní převážně ze starého domova (odchod sovětských vojáků, moravské lidové zvyky a muziky aj.) a z Podkarpatské Rusi, součásti předválečného Československa, země zastaveného času.

Značnou část života věnuje Dukát shromažďování starých přístrojů, především aut, v nichž nejezdí. Je umělcem jejich údržby. Na autě, v němž jezdí, opraví vždy jen to nejnutnější, aby se pak mohl těšit, co dalšího se zase pokazí. Namísto svého díla propaguje automobil Tatra, jehož aerodynamický tvar znamenal v roce 1934 jedinečný příspěvek automobilovému designu.

Osobnost Vojty Dukáta není nutným úvodem k jeho fotografiím, je snad jen vysvětlením jejich nedostatku. Fotografie se obejdou bez všeho vysvětlování. Jsou to nenápadné černobílé momentky (jejich autor říká, že nevidí barevně). Protože jsou nenápadné, člověk si dlouho nemusí uvědomit jejich zvláštnost. Snad nejvíc se liší od obvyklých děl fotožurnalismu, jsou snad ve všem jejich protipólem. Až na výjimky nereferují o faktickém dění, o senzacích a celebritách, nejsou ulovené ve chvatu. Jsou to klidné, vyvážené snímky, a je-li v nich drama, není na povrchu. Těmito rysy se liší i od expresivního stylu, který dominoval v šedesátých a ještě v sedmdesátých letech, tedy v době, kdy se utvářela Dukátova osobnost. Poté co fotografové jako William Klein, Josef Koudelka a další naučili diváky ve jménu naléhavého sdělení akceptovat provokativní záběry, výřezy s „uříznutými" figurami, deformace optikou, zrnitost zvětšenin atd., Dukát se vrátil nejen před tento styl, ale ještě hlouběji do minulosti.

Po určité době prohlížení Dukátových fotografií může být nápadné, že se odchylují od paradigmatu fotožurnalismu, formulovaného Robertem Capou: „Nejsou-li tvé fotografie dobré, nebyls dost blízko." Množství záběrů Vojty Dukáta, snad většina, je koncipována v uctivé vzdálenosti od pohyblivých složek zahlédnutého obrazu. Uctivé proto, že Dukát má ke spatřeným obrazům úctu a nechce narušit jejich autenticitu. (V době Dukátova dospívání byla autenticita, vlivem existencialismu, snad nejfrekventovanějším slovem. Avšak tehdy bylo její zárukou nitro umělce, u Dukáta je to sama skutečnost.) Pokud Dukát fotografuje z těsné blízkosti, znamená to, že neměl čas nebo prostor, kam ustoupit. Modernismus odmítl iluzivní umění 19. století, založené na idealistické představě (božího) celku světa. Dukát, vědomě či nevědomě, možná nechce nic menšího než vrátit se před moderní chaos k předchozímu řádu. V hranicích jeho původního domova to není tak neobvyklé, vždyť Josef Sudek udělal něco podobného v oboru statické fotografie.

Vojta Dukát tedy vykrajuje své záběry jako kusy dortu z harmonického celku světa, jehož existenci pociťuje navzdory všemu. Mimořádný důraz klade na výtvarnou dokonalost a současně přirozenost svých kompozic. Je konzervativním fotografem. Vyznění jeho fotografií je často lyrické. Tvary na jeho fotografiích bývají sametově hebké, obalené světlem pořádajícím svět.

Jaký je to svět? Nepochybně je to současný svět, fotografie ani jinou možnost nemá, ale není to současný svět spěchu, pracovního výkonu, konzumu atd. Po chvíli si divák asi začne uvědomovat, že v Dukátově světě chybí současná architektura, banky, moderní doprava a téměř vše, co charakterizuje dnešek. Naopak je v něm hodně minulosti tkvící v přítomnosti. Mizející starý způsob a starý pocit života. Některé fotografie z maloměst a vesnic skutečně mohou být matoucí, například na jihu existují nadčasové oděvy (sukně nebo kalhoty a bílá košile nebo halenka) a nadčasové činnosti (věšení prádla), takže záměna se sto let starou fotografií je dobře možná. Něco podobného platí pro snímky lidových zvyků a slavností. Dokumentaristé se vždy snažili zakonzervovat to, co pokračující civilizace odsoudila k zániku. U Dukáta k tomu přistupuje i úcta k předchozí historii jeho média, kterou se nesnaží překonat díly revolučně novými, nýbrž naopak se snaží zůstat co nejvíc pozadu, aby mohl klasikům s úctou hledět na záda a dělat fotografie, které by kdysi možná nové nebyly, ale dnes nové jsou.

Většina Dukátových fotografií neukazuje nic exotického. Jsou to záběry nejvšednější všednosti, zcela v duchu dominantních tradic umění v bývalém Československu. Nevšední je to, co fotograf z všednosti vybírá. Sám mluví o tom, že fotografuje samotu. Není to příliš přesné. Osamělí lidé na Dukátových fotografiích vždy sami sebe přesahují, protože je fotograf začlenil do vztahů k dalším věcem a lidem, do většího celku, který oni nevidí, protože nemohou vyjít ze sebe, aby se na sebe podívali. Obvykle si neuvědomují, jak je fotograf vidí, ale dodatečně snad vždy berou jeho obrazy za své, a my také. Vždyť kdo chce být sám, a kdo by nechtěl být součástí vyšší harmonie? Dukát připomíná starobylou roli uměleckých děl jako poslů útěchy a touhy po nápravě světa.

Antonín Dufek, 2001, 2013

Osip Mandelštam fotografie *

Někdy leží na březích nebrázděného moře, na úpatí neobydleného pohoří nebo uprostřed vyprahlé nížiny, kde už by člověk neočekával ani vísku či samotu, město.

Tato věta, jejíž mluvnický předmět stojí až úplně na konci (podobně jako u auta, které má motor umístěn na zadní nápravě), je úvodní větou románu Povstání v Guadalajaře od Jana Slauerhoffa. Vždycky jsem ji považoval za jednu z nejkrásnějších úvodních vět v naší literatuře, a i kdyby neměla sloužit jako úvodní věta, byla by to formule, před kterou se tají dech. Občas si na tuto větu vzpomenu, většinou spontánně, a několikrát se mi to také stalo, když jsem se na cestách dostal někam, kde by se člověk případně spokojil i s imaginárním městem. A v ojedinělém, zvláštním případě se pak ukáže, že takový druh měst skutečně existuje. Byl jsem jednou v Novgorodě, v Rusku, a tam široko daleko není vůbec nic, co by naznačovalo, že jste na cestě do Novgorodu. Ale totéž se vám stane v Itálii, kde některá města neleží na úpatí hor, ale jsou postavena na vrcholcích nehostinných pohoří, jako Cortona, Urbino, Peruggia.

A existuje ještě čtvrtá příležitost, která mě nutí myslet na Slauerhoffovu větu – když prohlížím některé fotografie Vojty Dukáta. Budu-li opatrně parafrázovat, dojdu přibližně k takovéto formulaci: někdy vznikne na okraji náměstí, které zůstalo úplně prázdné, na břehu jinak nenápadného kanálu, anebo v prostoru, kde bychom stěží očekávali přítomnost člověka, fotografie. S důrazem na onu první specifikaci, někdy, neboť jsou to obrazy, které při bližším ohledání mohl vytvořit jen Vojta Dukát.

Tím jsem se již přímo dotknul z mého pohledu ojedinělé vlastnosti Dukátova díla, totiž skutečnosti, že jeho tvorba nevykazuje žádnou podobnost s dílem jiných fotografů, a naopak, že si nedokážu vybavit žádného jiného fotografa, jehož fotografie by připomínaly ty Dukátovy. A to ani zdaleka. Dukátovo dílo se podobá nanejvýš fotografiím, které byste si, máte-li dostatek fantazie, mohli představit, anebo které byste, jste-li na to dost ješitní, sami chtěli vytvořit. Dukát je zcela svůj a pouze mimo oblast fotografie si dokážu vybavit jména některých umělců, jejichž pozice by se dala charakterizovat podobným způsobem. A možná je příznačné, že se přitom vybaví (alespoň mně) především poezie: básně Emily Dickinsonové se podobají jen jiným básním Emily Dickinsonové. Osip Mandelštam se nepodobá nikomu jinému, a jediné, co jeho epigoni dokázali, je, že se mu ani podobat nelze. Ale abychom nechodili tak daleko, poezie Elisabeth Eybersové, psaná v afrikánštině, se vzpírá každému pokusu vytvářet asociace s jinou poezií. Vždyť přece: „Waneer die erts geskei is van die steen / moet dit gesmelt, ontsmet word en gesmee / voor dit in suiwerheid tevoorskyn tree" („Když z kamene kyz vytěžíš / vytav ho, vyčisti a vykovej / pak jeho ryzost se vyjeví").

Suiwerheid, ryzost je podle mého názoru další Dukátova vlastnost, přičemž ale podotýkám, že tento pojem bývá často zneužíván a že jen málo hodnocení je tak pochybných jako hodnocení, které se zakládá na autentičnosti – autentického a zároveň naprosto nanicovatého je na světě spousta. Abych vysvětlil jasněji, co myslím čistotou ve fotografii Vojty Dukáta, musím nejprve vyprávět příběh.

Jednou jsem byl z důvodů, které zde nejsou důležité, v Petrohradě. Sněžilo, mrzlo, bylo snad dvanáct stupňů pod nulou a byla mi zima. Usmyslel jsem si udělat něco, čemu jsem se při dřívějších návštěvách v Rusku vždycky vyhýbal: rozhodl jsem se, že si koupím beranici. Zeptal jsem se jednoho Rusa, který byl v naší společnosti, kde bych si ji mohl nejlépe opatřit, a on mě odkázal na obchodní dům na Něvském prospektu u mostu Aničkova. Podrobnosti nejsou podstatné, jde o scénu, která se mi otevřela, když jsem překročil práh. Tedy nejprve podlaha. Ta byla tak jako podlaha každého obchodu v Petrohradě v lednu pokryta vrstvou blátivého a zpola roztátého sněhu, přičemž si hned uvědomíte, že jste na to po celou dobu, kdy jste nebyli v Rusku, nikdy ani na vteřinu nepomysleli. A potom sám interiér: zbytečně velký prostor, veškerá omítka špinavá a popraskaná, létací dveře zavěšené na opotřebených pantech a něco jako pult z tmavohnědého dřeva, od něhož jako z přídě lodi shlížela asi stoletá žena na tu nakupující sebranku. Celá tato symfonie absurdních detailů, jejichž žalostnou přesnost jsem už zapomněl, mi ale zároveň připomněly (ještě naléhavěji než při přistání letadla), že jsem v Rusku. Koupil jsem si svou beranici. Za tři sta tisíc rublů.

Zanedlouho nato, jednou v poledne, mně Hripsimé Visser v Městském muzeu moderního umění v Amsterdamu ukázala výběr z fotografií Vojty Dukáta, který právě prováděla.

Jako všichni ostatní jsem jeho dílo znal jen povrchně. Zřídka bylo vystaveno nebo publikováno. Jeden z prvních exemplářů, které jsem viděl, vznikl v roce 1985 v tehdejším Leningradě. Jsou na něm hodiny, které od okamžiku, kdy byla fotografie pořízena, ukazují tři čtvrtě na jednu, pult a za ním ruskou děžurnou, která bedlivě sleduje dění. Na fotografii je nejasně vidět něco z ulice za skleněnými létacími dveřmi. Ve dveřích jsou dvě ženy, jedna jde dovnitř, druhá vychází ven. Nic víc než několik nahodilých skutečností, ale bylo to, jako bych zaslechl první takt symfonie, kterou jsem dávno neslyšel. A tento první takt stačil, aby se vyplnilo místo v hudební paměti, ne v reálném čase, ale doslova v mžiku: byla to budova, kde jsem před nedávnem byl, jiného roku, za jiných okolností, ale se stejnou vůní, se stejným měnivým šerosvitem, stejným elektrizujícím dopadem na vnímání. Jinak řečeno: stejný pocit autentičnosti.

To však je poměrně jednoduchý příklad a musíme poděkovat především náhodě, že umožnila si ho ověřit na základě osobní zkušenosti. Situace bude o hodně složitější u mnoha z těch Dukátových obrazů, které, dalo by se říct, se k nám dostávají z druhé ruky, a nebo u těch, které se zcela odtrhly od svého důvěrného prostředí. A snad zvlášť extremním příkladem je jedna Dukátova fotografie, kterou vytvořil v roce 1979 v Curychu, na které jsou žena a muž v jakési kavárně a kouří. Podivné je – alespoň podle mě je to podivné –, že muž má nalakované nehty. Jsou na obraze jasně rozeznatelné jako tmavší body, mají dokonce svůj vlastní individuální lesk. Všechno ostatní, zdá se, bylo ponecháno jakoby mlhavé, místnost sama, výraz ženiny tváře, poloha ve které sedí a nakonec i význam, který se dá tomuto obrazu přisoudit. A přece není o nic méně opravdový než fotografie interiéru v Petrohradě.

Avšak jak je tomu s významem? Teď narazíme na stejně nezničitelný jako záhadný automatismus, který nás vede k tomu, že se fotografiím, třeba i neostrým, triviálním a pomíjivým, snažíme připsat nějaký význam. Je to skoro nutkání. Někdo si dal tu práci, že zachytil určitou situaci, a to samo o sobě už vytváří premisu, ontologický imperativ, který musí vést k víceméně konkretním důsledkům: co to vyjadřuje, co se za tím skrývá, proč fotografie vznikla, otázky tohoto druhu. Každá fotografie nutí k tomu, napsat pod ni titulek, a v této souvislosti je zajímavé, že – jak potvrzuje výzkum – čtenáři novin věnují víc času tomu, aby na sebe nechali působit obsah popisek pod fotografiemi, než aby se pokusili přečíst samotnou fotografii. Taková je praxe i na výstavách, v muzeích jsou popisky, nebo snad lépe řečeno: jména nalezišť k nim příslušejících fotografií vytištěny na jedné stránce o formátu A4.

V prostoru připomínajícím kostel vidíme ženu oblečenou do jakéhosi pyžama s květinovým motivem. Vedle ní sedí u stolku s krajkovým ubrusem vážně se tvářící muž. Vedle něho sedí ještě jeden muž v černém saku. Na klíně má něco jako koňskou houni. Pod ní zahlédnete jeho bosé nohy.

Napříč obrazem jde muž. Pod paží nese zřejmě těžký předmět vyhlížející jako dveře. V popředí je dívka v šatech, které jsou jí trochu velké, která objímá paží okolo ramen starou ženu. Obě se dívají do objektivu, stará paní poněkud zamlženě.

Muž leží s hlavou na stole a spí. Na stole je šálek od čaje, sklenice a popelník. V pozadí se nějaký chodec dívá oroseným oknem dovnitř. Má tmavé brýle, jeho obličej připomíná Prima Leviho.

V místnosti s kostkovaným kobercem stojí muž a žena. Není dobře jasné, zda tančí, anebo jestli se žena právě chystá vlepit muži pohlavek. V pozadí pod monumentálním schodištěm dělá žena v dlouhých kalhotách taneční kroky.

Čtyři fotografie. Příslušné texty: Západní Samoa 1973, Oporto 1979, Curych 1979, Blackpool 1978. Pozoruhodné je, že texty jsou i bez ohledu na svůj uniformní vzhled téměř zcela zaměnitelné. Fotografie z Curychu mohla vzniknout – tak to aspoň vypadá – stejně dobře v Blackpoolu a fotografie z roku 1973 stejně tak v roce 1979. Zčásti je to tím, že Dukátovo dílo je téměř zcela nadčasové (v tom smyslu, že jeho fotografie neobsahují žádný odkaz na dobu, kdy byly vytvořeny). Dále také proto, že Dukát fotografuje situace, které nenesou žádnou příliš specifickou pečeť, jako například anekdotu nebo angažovanost.

Mnohdy tam, kde chybí specifičnost, nastupuje místo ní symbolika. Je to postup, který se hojně uplatňuje u všech pokusů učinit fotografii po umělecké stránce salonfähig, od Alfreda Stieglitze až k André Kertészovi, od Alberta Rengera-Patzsche až po Nobuyoschi Araki.

Myslím, že bychom zacházeli příliš daleko, kdybychom v Dukátově případě mluvili o symbolických nebo symbolistických fotografiích. K symbolu vždy patří skrytá dohoda týkající se vztahu mezi znakem a tím, co znak symbolizuje. K tomu, aby se zabránilo přílišnému zmatku, je zapotřebí určitý systém. A je tu, samozřejmě, interpretace, takže lze alespoň symbol úspěšně dekódovat.

Můj dojem je, že Dukát zvolil zcela jinou cestu a že nejlepší způsob, jak přiřadit jeho fotografiím smysl, spočívá v tom, co bych ve zkratce nazval „obraz jako takový".

Připouštím, že to moc pěkný termín není, nemám ale prozatím žádný lepší. K jeho objasnění učiňme krátkou odbočku do dějin literatury.

Na začátku tohoto století vznikl v ruské poezii proud, který byl označován poněkud problematickým pojmem akméismus. Tento termín pochází z řeckého slova akmé, což znamená vrchol nebo nejvyšší bod, tedy vrchol hory. Akméisté (k nejznámějším patřili Anna Achmatovová, Nikolaj Gumiljov a Osip Mandelštam) byli toho názoru, že u symbolistů, jejich předchůdců, dospěl jazyk tím, že každé slovo může nabývat libovolného počtu nových, symbolických významů, k takovému zmatení, že je zapotřebí obnovit zaměření na spojitost mezi slovem a věcí. Jazyk musí být tak říkajíc očištěn od veškeré kolísavosti a mystiky, od veškeré verbální inflace. Slova ve svém původním smyslu musí být znovu umístěna na vrchol, musí být naostřena a zapsána. Jde o slovo jako takové, rusky slovo kak takóvoje. A tato prvotní podoba poukazuje především na konkrétní, ryzí, chceme-li, pozemskou skutečnost. V jednom ze svých manifestů to akméisté formulovali takto:

> „Spor mezi akméismem a symbolismem je především sporem o tento svět o jeho zvuky, jeho barvy, jeho formy, jeho váhu a čas, je to spor o naši planetu Zemi. Pro akméisty je růže znovu krásná tím, jaká je, svými květy, svou vůní a barvou, a ne pro svou pomyslnou podobnost s mystickou láskou nebo čímkoli jiným."

Dva příklady, abychom osvětlili onen druh jednoduchosti, o niž akméisté usilovali. Achmatovová napsala báseň, kde říká, když popisuje svoji nervozitu, že se pokouší strčit pravou ruku do levé rukavice. A od Mandelštama pochází strofa, kde říká: „Sedíme v kuchyni, ty a já / Sladce voní bílý kerosín." Nervozitu není třeba dále popisovat. Rukavice a kerosín, „slovo jako takové", jsou jako palivo dostatečné.

V dějinách fotografie je znám nekonečný počet výroků fotografů, kteří se domnívali, že pomocí svého média musí nalézat pravdu. „Fotografie je má vášeň, hledání pravdy má posedlost," napsal americký fotograf Alfred Stieglitz. Samo o sobě na tom není nic zvláštního, někdy se tvrdívá, že každý směr v umění, každý -ismus, jakkoliv abstraktní nebo neurčitý, má tendenci vydávat se za realismus. Používání jazyka se tím ovšem rozhodně nezjednoduší. Velký anglický filosof Michael Dummett napsal před dvaceti lety knihu s pozoruhodným názvem Pravda a jiné záhady. Už jen proto je pěkné a dobré, že se čas od času objeví umělci, básníci a fotografové, kteří alespoň vzbuzují dojem, že opět chtějí začít od začátku. Od slova nebo obrazu v jejich nejčistší a nejvíce odzbrojující podobě. Jinak řečeno, od obrazu jako takového.

Dlouhý stín romantiky se postaral o to, že právě ty nejjednodušší reprezentace mohou být jen stěží vnímány, aniž by ten, kdo je vnímá, v sobě nepocítil jisté vzedmutí sklonů k nějaké formě dojetí. Často se dokonce vyskytuje něco jako aktivní ochota nechat se dojímat. Všichni ten pocit známe, když jde o archeologické předměty, zejména, pocházejí-li z každodenního kontextu: mozaiky v římských lázních, přezka od šatů, náhodný nápis, thou, silent form, dost tease us out of thought, as doth Eternity. Je to ono výsostně romantické srovnání na které se odvolává Keats ve své slavné ódě na řeckou urnu: Beauty is truth, truth is beauty. Jedná se o tutéž identifikaci, k níž téměř o dvě stě let později stále ještě dochází v mnohých myslích. Zachází to dokonce tak daleko, že i předměty, které nebyly přímo vykopány, ale které jsou nějakým způsobem archaické nebo exotické a zároveň každodenní, udeří na romantickou strunu. Nazval bych to turistickou variantou: zajeďte si do některého zapadlého kouta na okraji důvěrně známého světadílu, do Portugalska, do Istanbulu, na předměstí Moskvy, na sever Skotska, a všude najdete nějakého rybáře, čističe bot, továrničku nebo zříceninu, nějaké téma, které dokáže způsobit, aby co je běžné, vypadalo jako něco zdánlivě mimořádného. K tomu, aby vznikla fotografie, pak stačí stisknout knoflík. Někdy dokonce ani to není nutné. V Toskánsku se prodávají plakáty složené snad ze stovky malých fotografií toskánských domovních dveří, které svou příslovečnou malebností dokáží beze zbytku ukojit romantickou zálibu v klišé. Lidé na dovolené, kteří plakáty kupují, si ve svém poblouznění snad ani neuvědomují, že si domů neodvážejí pravdivý obraz, ale pouze podmíněný symbol Toskánska.

Vojta Dukát si pro své působení na pomezí mezi hodinou psa a vlka skutečně nevybral nejpohodlnější prostor. Dokázal od sebe odvrhnout balast více než jednoho století dějin fotografie. Pochopil, že specifičnost na sebe často až příliš často bere podobu symbolu. Ignoroval hřmot doby a vydal se znovu na cestu hledání inherentní poezie fotografického obrazu.

Pod pomerančovníkem stojí děvče. Aspoň si myslíte, že je to pomerančovník. Zdá se, že se dívá do objektivu aparátu. Vlevo ve dveřích stojí starší muž opřený o zárubeň. Kouří cigaretu. Nad dveřmi je upevněné číslo domu, číslo 6. Za 600 let bude děvče stále ještě hledět do objektivu, stejně tak jako na jedněch hodinách v Petrohradě bude pořád ještě tři čtvrtě na jednu.

V Bolívii stojí v kulečníkovém sále žena. Je sama. Drží v rukou tágo, její postoj je téměř dokonale symetrický. Dvěma dveřmi se otevírá pohled na ulici. Je vidět další dvoje dveře a okapovou rouru. Na kulečníku leží ještě druhé tágo a bílá koule.

V Krakově stojí litinová pouliční lucerna, v pozadí je opuštěný tovární komplex. Kolem jde chlapec, ještě o ničem neví. Snaží se udržet ve vzduchu kopací míč.

V Burgosu ve Španělsku kráčí po ulici dvě slepé ženy v zimnících. Mají hole a jedna žena má na řemínku kolem krku kazetový magnetofon. Co se v nich odehrává, ví snad jen Bůh, ale v každém případě budí dojem, že se rozhodly udělat si příjemný den.

Pod oválným portrétem panenky Marie stojí čtyři ženy neurčitého věku. Polsko 1982. Musí to být nedávno, kdy Wojcziech Jaruzelski vyhlásil výjimečný stav. Čekají, ale není vidět na co. Jedna z žen zvedla levou nohu a opírá si ji, nebo možná tře, o holeň pravé nohy. Co to vyjadřuje? Co taková fotografie znamená? A jsou tyto otázky ještě vůbec na místě?

V komentáři napsaném v roce 1995 pro výstavu v Praze Vojta Dukát říká:

> „Je dobré a velmi vzrušující osmělit se, přesto však s pokorou pozorovat obrazy v okamžiku jejich vzniku, přibližovat se k nim, zkoušet a alespoň několikrát v životě i zachytit ty zdánlivě dokonalé, ty, které chceme vidět, které vlastně již známe a které se, byť v stále menší míře, z každodenních situací občas vynoří.“

Je to vyjádřeno subtilně a téměř mimochodem: ty, které vlastně již známe.

Jedná se o onu vyšší formu symboliky, v níž někdo díky výjimečné schopnosti vidění je schopen vydobýt významy zpět ze skutečnosti. Je to vzpomínka na to, na čem nebylo nutné se domlouvat.

Melchior de Wolff

* Proslov Melchiora de Wolffa přednesný ve Stedelijk Muzeu v Amsterdamu u příležitosti předání Ceny Capi-Lux Alblas Prijs za dlouhodobý přínos na poli vizuální komunikace, kterou Vojta Dukát obdržel v roce 1997.

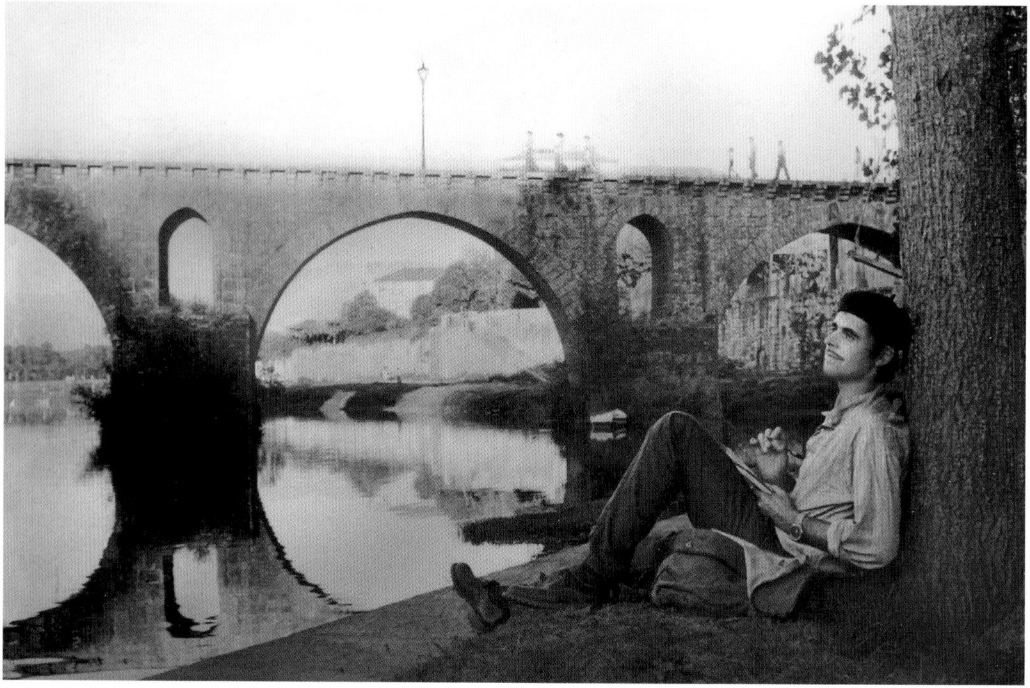

Vojta Dukát, Ponte de Barca, Portugal / Portugalsko, 1976, photo / foto Miloš Stejskal

Dva eseje Vojty Dukáta

Je dobré a velmi vzrušující osmělit se, přesto však s pokorou pozorovat obrazy v okamžiku jejich vzniku, přibližovat se k nim, zkoušet a alespoň několikrát v životě i zachytit ty zdánlivě dokonalé, ty, které chceme vidět, které vlastně již známe a které se, byť v stále menší míře, z každodenních situací občas vynoří. Spatřit alespoň na chvíli i ty méně dokonalé může být obohacením, podobně jako čerpáme z obrazů, které potkali a zachránili jiní, bylo-li nám dovoleno do nich nahlédnout. Žijí pak dál, s námi, jsou dobrou potravou, je na ně spolehnutí, můžeme s nimi obcovat, léčí a nikdy nezklamou. Doufám jen, že je nebolí vznik proti své vůli, že často znamenají, co nechtěly, či to, co jejich příchod ozáří v spletitých labyrintech našich srdcí.

Vracím se také často k těm situacím, které unikly, kde chybělo jen málo a mohly nastat, kdy se nezastavilo vše najednou... a nestaly se obrazem.[1]

A právě z těch situací:

„kdy vše náhle na okamžik ztichne
jak na místech, kde nezpívají ptáci,
kde se však zde či někde v okolí
přec jen, jen tak malušenko, cosi tetelí"...[2]

se pak stávají obrazy, v nichž čas má setrvačnost a třpytí se, i když již dávno zanikly. Řekněte mi prosím, jak je to dlouho, co odjel vlak? Bylo to moc, moc pěkné? Dlí krásno jen v očích obdivovatele? Je pravda, pokud vůbec existuje, tak spletitá a skrytá jako koruna z peří? Tak podobně se snad kdysi tázaly, hledajíce i zbytky obrazů své éry, zádumčivé bytosti v dobách již dávno minulých, kdy ještě žili klasici. Naštěstí se nenarodili později, nezanechali by nám pomůcky ke zpytování svědomí a provždy krásná a mocná zaklínadla...

...Dívat se nemusí být vždy bez poranění. Potřebujeme neustále nové obrazy, nejsou-li dokonalejší než ty, které jsme kdy spatřili a již tak dlouho vlastníme? Dokážeme je zavčas odložit, jestliže vycítíme, že k nám nepatří? Je stále těžší dívat se, aniž by nám vše něco nepřipomínalo, bohužel většinou něco lepšího. Mám dobré cvičení: Na počátku bylo slovo... zdálo se, že postačí:[3] Byl pozdní večer – první máj – večerní máj – byl lásky čas – dívejme se ale až za jamb, trochu dál, k jezeru – kde ku lásce zval hrdliččin hlas – kde borový zaváněl háj...[4]

...nebo od nás:

„boly časy boly, ale sa minuly
a po malej chvíli mineme sa aj my,
keď sa my mineme, mine sa krajina,
jako by odpadél vršek z rozmarýna...“ [5]

a tato:

„strom o strom sa bije, ftáča preletuje,
naša láska taká je...“ [5]

Co jsme právě viděli, je rajská zahrada, tento pohled překoná snad až jen vstup do ní samé... tím bychom si měli vymývat mysl každý den. Tyto obrazy, hlavně ty nejstarší, dnes nikomu nepůjčujme, mohly by se někam zašantročit a nevrátit se; stali bychom se pak prázdnou nádobou a multimédia by nás slupla jako malinu natotata... A vidět pak už jen císařovy nové šaty? ...pak už nepomůže, pane Gottlieb, vůbec nic, ani svěcená voda, ani žádný šém, pak už ani není komu... Pane Gottlieb, neskákejte z okna – bydlíte v přízemí! Něco podobného už tvrdil Rilke, no a vidíte, od té doby byly už jen dvě války, potom komunisti, pak ti bývalí, bolševník, šaty s nápisy a baseballové čepice a teď multimédia – ale vždy bylo a vždy bude možné spatřit také jiskru v očích milované bytosti... chvilku počkáme, než to přejde... Poďte, mezi tím si zazpíváme:

„...chvála bohu, že sem sa narodil,
že sem svojich mladých roků užil,
měl jsem v světě ty jedny jediné,
odešly ně, nebudu mět jiné.
Rozpomeň sa, ó člověče, na to,
že nic nejsi, jen popel a blato.
Keď ty prídeš na súd pánů Pána,
nepomůže ti výmluva žádná...“ [5]

Poznámky

1 Úryvky z připravované sbírky textů T. S. Gottlieba Obrazy a slova (záznamy rozhovorů s Vojtou Dukátem), připravuje nakladatelství Lucid, Brno.
2 Úryvek z básně T. S. Gottlieba „Dancing Rays“ (Tančící paprsky) ze sbírky Quiet Friendships (Tichá přátelství), nakladatelství M. Kalisch, N. Y. C., USA 1974, překlad Vojta Dukát.
3 Výňatky z korespondence Vojta Dukát / T. S. Gottlieb.
4 Úryvek z básně K. H. Máchy – Máj.
5 Úryvky z moravských lidových písní.

Text z katalogu výstavy Orbis Fictus – nová média v současném umění, Valdštejnská jízdárna Praha, Kurátor – Keiko Sei, připravilo Sorosovo centrum současného umění, Praha, Česká republika 1995.

Nejdůležitější je vědět, co nefotit,[1] jestliže, ať už je to cokoli, co později zůstane na papíře, bez ohledu na to, co vše mohlo znamenat předtím, než se tam dostalo, se nestane čímsi plochým a ohraničeným, něčím, co se snaží oddělit se svými okraji od prostoru, kde se nyní proti své vůli nachází, kam nepatří – a nevydá ze sebe něco, co ještě stále o nás jeví zájem a je na oplátku dosud hodno byť jen letmého pohledu, který však okamžitě dává tušit hutnější, komplexní, skutečný obraz v pozadí – což není ta věc, na kterou se díváte...

Ten papír, to je jen fotografie.

Tím myslím: být tím něčím jen přitahováni... nezmocňovat se nebo nedej Bůh analyzovat a verbalizovat – to, co tam vlastně není... Jediný přípustný způsob, jak komentovat obrazy, je Ticho..., nebo nanejvýš nesrozumitelný šepot, ozvěna jakás... odrážející striktně soukromý šelest vědomí, který někdy může vyústit i v samovolný povzdech: Aaah... jež, kdyby se dalo přeložit, by ve filosofické rovině překonalo i hodnotu již tak vzrušujícího, na první pohled zdánlivě logického poznatku:

Znovu a znovu se moře zdá být tak obrovské, klidné a nekonečně nekonečné... skoro jako... jako... jako moře.[2]

Prožitek, o který by v dnešní době bohužel nebylo vhodné pokoušet se příliš často dělit s ostatními na veřejnosti nebo zkoušet jej uveřejnit na stránkách prestižních uměleckých časopisů pod vlastním jménem, tedy pokud by se nejednalo o jedince se sebevražednými sklony... Všichni dobře známe podstatu onoho šepotu o moři, není ničím novým, stává se však lepší a lepší pokaždé, když... byť při různých příležitostech a z různých důvodů – dojdeme opět ke stejnému závěru: pak se zrodí „Nové“, hlubší, zkušenější „Staré“. To je to „Nové“, které, kdybychom se o ně dělili s jinými ve větší míře, by mohlo být tak potřebnou útěchou a ozdravným přínosem pro lidstvo i jistým odškodněním za bolest způsobenou výsledky úporných mozkových aktivit jiného druhu, jejichž výdobytky nám dnes nabízejí muzea soudobého umění a přinášejí umělecké časopisy, které s ním obcují... Mohlo by mít onen zmírňující uklidňující efekt, který se nás zmocní, pohlížíme-li na moře: tak nekonečně obrovské, klidné a věčné, jako to vše – co tam vlastně není, sloučeno dohromady –, to, co jsme někdy mohli tušit i za některými plochými, ohraničenými povrchy – a co v nás znovu a znovu vyvolalo pocity vyrovnanosti a uklidnění, kterým se tak rádi blahovolně oddáváme, jelikož jsou nám často tak dobře známé jako ty, jež nás ovládnou, díváme-li se na moře, které se opět: Znovu a znovu zdá být...

Je politováníhodné, že tyto pocity, a to nejen ve mně, až příliš často nevyvolává něco, co vzniká pod umělým tlakem „inovátorství za každou cenu“ vytvářeným, zdá se, především těmi kurátory dychtivě toužícími po nových objevech... ve spojení s v tomto ohledu nebezpečně vysokou rychlostí výměny informací i prostou existencí časových pásem. Někde je ještě dnes..., ale jinde to již znamená včera... a pak již může být na prvenství pozdě... a celý svět by se zhroutil.

To co je pak obvykle označováno jako provokativně progresivní, je však jen okatě rádoby odvážné, nevyzrále bezdůvodně rozpitvané, zůstává povětšinou záměrně fragmentární... pokouší se opět již z dalšího tabu strhnout oponu tajemství a zcela jistě „velmi veliké ambiciózní něco“. To, co lze často jen obtížně vměstnat nejen do muzeí samých s jejich povětšinou starosvětskými, pro potřeby současných tvůrců často neprozřetelně poddimenzovanými portály, ale především posléze bezbolestně a bez intimidace vtěsnat i do většiny – daleko vyšší nároky si kladoucích myslí, těch – schopných rozlišovat, kteří, pokud vůbec, pak jen sporadicky dychtí po tom, co již dávno v minulosti vešlo ve známost jako: každodenní, tuctové, vizuálně nesamonosné konceptuální foto-monumentálno.

Nicméně: dívejte se nadále na to, co „je“ kolem vás, snažte se však spatřit a doufejte, že zachytíte jen to, co chcete, aby zůstalo, až se „teď“ promění v „bylo“ a stane se navždy pouhým – nejlépe nepříliš velkým „placatým obdélníkem“... na jehož povrchu se však „byť jen z mála – stává více“ a může, pokud je samo schopno zpětného pohybu, takto opět nabýt, nejlépe však i překonat původní dimenze toho, co jste si přáli, aby – a doufám, že především pro nás – na závěr zůstalo. To, co není..., ale je však tak často předmětem zájmu mnoha..., je možno zviditelnit jen skrze to – co je... Pak může to, co je, ustoupit tomu, co není... pak se z více může opět stát méně, nebo nic – byl-li to váš skutečný záměr, aniž by výsledek snahy zviditelnit neviditelné musel být později opět „zneviditelněn“. Buď všudypřítomným dotěrným egem umělce, neustále zaclánějícím ve výhledu, či zahalen, obklopen a permanentně podpírán pochybným umělým verbálním lešením... z pera a ochotně dodaným osobami, které se, tak jako ona lešení v závěru, stávají nedílnou součástí, ne-li dokonce dominantní složkou takto ošetřených uměleckých počinů, přičemž tímto často velmi ambiciozním Verbálnem dále znečišťují již beztak značně zamořenou doménu Vizuálna.

V případě že onen, byť jen nepatrný zlomek toho, „co kdysi bylo kolem vás“, je ještě stále hoden alespoň letmého pohledu, pak v nás může dle vlastní potřeby a míry – vámi v nás vyvolaného momentálního zjitření smyslů – naším vlastním přičiněním nabýt víc než monumentálních rozměrů, o kterých se vám ani nesnilo... poměřitelných však výhradně jen v jednotkách Aaah..., dosud nestandardizovaných velmi proměnných jednotkách intenzity vizuálních prožitků úměrných jen našim vlastním potřebám v daném okamžiku.

Monumentálních rozměrů?

Ano, avšak v o něco pokornějším slova smyslu... jen natolik, aby „monumentálno" námi vytvořených „vnitřních obrazů" nabylo jen té velikosti, se kterou si ještě troufáme být konfrontováni... jen natolik, aby míra hustoty vizuálních prožitků byla ještě smysluplným obohacujícím přínosem v přepočtu na cm^4 onoho tajemného, někdy i čtyřdimenzionálního imaginárního prostoru, kde tajemné „Je ne sais quoi"[3] zvolilo své sídlo. Minimálně však: Aaah na N / imaginární $cm^2 > cm^2$ nosiče.[4]

Pokud jste ale až dosud ještě ani jednou – promáčeni potem – nebyli vytrženi ze sna, ve kterém vám bylo dáno jen v mžiku zahlédnout něco, co je vám vlastně známé, co jste však až dosud ještě nikdy nespatřili v živé podobě, ani nevěda, že jste vlastně v očekávání, ale Vládce snů, který vás tím letmým pohledem obdařil, rozhodl, že si ještě nezasloužíte onen prst, kterým se mačká spoušť... a už to bylo pryč... pryč navždy... a odteď budete muset s tímto ztraceným obrazem žít sami, navždy, na věky věků, až do konce času... plně si vědomi, že nemůžeme vědět, co jsme ztratili, dokud to neztratíme, ale že to nejprve musíme získat...

Nekupujte si foťák...!

Neuvidíte přes něj nic víc, než jen to, co je... Je to tak prosté a můžete tím hodně ušetřit... a v případě, že pravým důvodem k výměně pyžama té noci byly jen vaše nezkrotné ambice, bude to i nejlepší zárukou, že někdy v budoucnu mé oko nezavadí o vaše zcela jistě velmi veliká, velice kontemplativní Nic s A4 po jejich boku s vysvětlením, co vše se vám tak promyšleně podařilo přede mnou utajit, až na to: Proč?..., jelikož Proč ne? se stalo standardní odpovědí. Skutečný důvod jejich existence, který – i bezobsažná díla ho v sobě musí obsahovat – se nám však sám nikdy nevyjeví, je od počátku koncipován tak, aby nebyl nikdy pochopen... tedy, pokud nebudeme zkoumat jeho integritu v širším kontextu jednoho dne... Těm, kteří se dosud ještě ptají: Proč se mám na to dívat?, se dostane okamžité odpovědi pohledem na vašeho Anděla Strážného, do jehož stáje budete muset náležet, kterak on, tanče ve světle reflektorů, zviditelňuje skutečnou podstatu věci, připomínaje vám pravidla parazitní symbiózy KIN[5] a nám ona nepříliš neposkvrněná početí těchto nečistých soužití, jejichž plody jsou tak často předkládány nevinným duším, které se dosud ještě „nevzdaly veškerých nadějí" při vstupu do novodobých katedrál „Toho, co vůbec není".

Netruchlete však, cesta ke spáse je stále otevřená...

Jděte... dokud je ještě čas... a naučte se třeba... řekněme... uvařit dobrou polévku!... třeba tu, co se dělá z kyselého mléka, čerstvého kopru, kmínu, brambor, soli, pár kapek octa, trochy mouky, možná trochy cukru a natvrdo uvařeného vajíčka... toho s tím pěkným žlutým žloutkem.[6] Je krásná na pohled, teplá a má velkou výživnou hodnotu..., tak tu medicínu ale hlavně nezhltejte sami, pomyslete nejprve na ty, kteří ji nejvíce potřebují... nechte proto vašemu Andělu Strážnému tu větší půlku a nezapomeňte mu k tomu dát recept...

Tímto počinem se stanete okamžitě navždy SLAVNÝMI a lidstvo na vás bude po zásluze s vděčností vzpomínat až do samého konce času...

To vám slibuji! Dobrou noc.

Vojta Dukát, 2002, 2012

Poznámky

1 Výňatky z textů Vojty Dukáta na téma: Profesionální intelektualizace a glorifikace neumětelství, kapitola: „Čím nekrmit vašeho Anděla Strážného" (© Vojta Dukát, 2002). Výňatky byly v roce 2002 autorem poskytnuty k využití jako dodatek k textu „Nejdůležitější je vědět, co nefotit" z pera PhDr. Antonína Dufka o Vojtovi Dukátovi z roku 2001. Doplněno v roce 2012 výňatky z interview Aleše Vašíčka s Vojtou Dukátem. Aleš Vašíček, M. A. Visual Thesis, The role of a curator in the exhibition making process, Role kurátora v průběhu přípravy výstav; Pedagog: Bas Vroege; Supervisor: Prof. Susan Meiselas, Leidenská universita, Leiden, Nizozemí, 2010.

2 Zdroj: text doprovázející kreslený vtip zobrazující pravděpodobně „Mladou služku při pohledu na moře". Dukátova interpretace původní kresby nemusí odpovídat tomu, co mohl mít její autor na mysli při jejím zhotovení. Text použitý v tomto pojednání v souvislosti s výše uvedeným kresleným vtipem je Dukátova volná interpretace původní verze textu, který si již přesně nepamatuje. Vzpomíná si jen, jak silně na něho tehdy zapůsobil a působí dodnes. Zveřejněno v Literárních novinách v ČSSR v roce +/–1968.

3 „Je ne sais quoi" – ono neuchopitelné něco.

4 Aaah na N / imaginární cm2 > cm2 nosiče © Vojta Dukát, 2012.

5 KIN: Kunst Industrie Normen, EU; AIN: Art Industry Norms, USA, Normy uměleckého průmyslu EU, USA, (©Vojta Dukát, 2001).

6 Umění kuchařské: velmi jednoduchý recept na: na pohled krásnou, dobrou a výživnou koprovou polévku, dle autorovy babičky, paní Jenovéfy Volánkové, Brno.

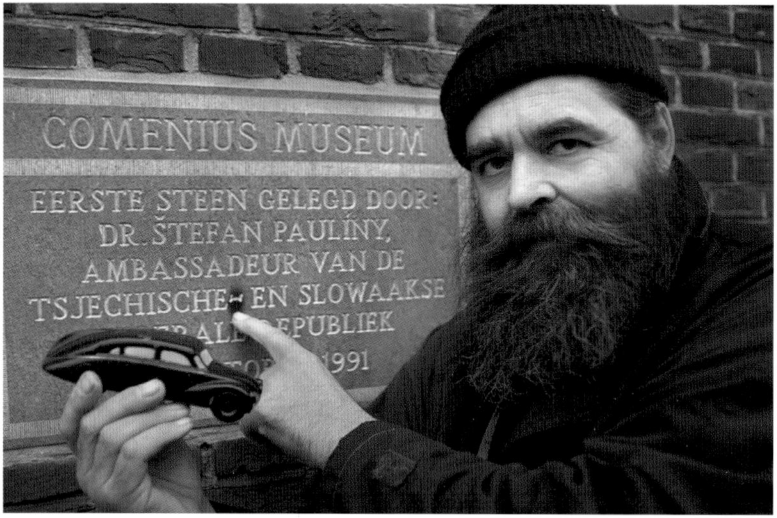

Vojta Dukát (with a model of the Tatra 87) touches the hyphen between the Czech and the Slovak Republics on the memorial plaque in the Comenius Museum, Naarden. The hyphen here symbolizes the country of his origin – Moravia. After being touched by many thousands of visitors, the hyphen has acquired a meaningful, dignified, and lasting shine that Moravia, considering the many contributions made by outstanding figures of Moravian descent in various professions on a worldwide scale throughout history, rightfully deserves. Not only on a memorial plaque in a foreign country, but also, indeed mainly, in today's disparagingly all-embracing Czech Republic, which systematically czechifies non-Czech citizens and all past and present contributions by people of other ethnicities.

Vojta Dukát (s modelem Tatry 87) se na pamětní desce v Muzeu Jana Amose Komenského v Naardenu dotýká pomlčky mezi Českou a Slovenskou republikou, symbolizující zde zemi jeho původu – Moravu. Pomlčky, která doteky mnoha tisíců návštěvníků získala významný, důstojný a trvalý lesk, jaký si Morava, vzhledem k dlouhodobému celosvětovému přínosu mnoha vynikajících osobností různých profesí původem z Moravy, po právu zaslouží. Nejen na pamětní desce v cizině, ale především v dnešní přezíravě všeobjímající, ne-české občany a veškeré minulé i soudobé přínosy příslušníků jiných národností systematicky počešťující České republice.

Tatra dle Dukáta *

Spolupráce, vynalézavost a řemeslné umění příslušníků různých národností podílejících se na syntéze elegance a vzrušujícího, důmyslného inženýrství v bývalém Česko–Slovensku s jeho epicentrem na Moravě, této nejprůmyslovější části bývalého Rakousko-Uherského impéria, byla jedinečným a dosud nepřekonaným přínosem v automobilovém designu. Stála u zrodu nesmírně ušlechtilého objektu Tatra 77 – omamné, nadpozemské krásy nejvyššího řádu, jíž byl tento nadnášen a zázračně poháněn vpřed, nepodléhaje všudypřítomným přírodním vlivům a fyzikálním zákonům. Tatra 77 sublimovala z obyčejného automobilu vyrobeného z hmoty v symbol „všeho dobrého, co má teprve přijít" odtud, co její tři světlomety vyzařující fotony až za nekonečno napříč pochmurnou temnotou pozůstatků poválečné světové krize ozařovaly – onen obrovský prostor, který byl tehdy ještě nazýván Budoucností. Sestoupení Tatry 77 na Zem v roce 1934 způsobilo dosud nepochopitelné zpomalení expanze vesmíru a okamžité zhutnění všech k tomuto bodu v čase lidstvu známých hodnot – a tím donutilo 3. tisíciletí k jeho příchodu do předválečného Česko–Slovenska o 67 let dříve než ve zbytku světa... Prototyp Tatra V570 z roku 1933 byl kopírován jako KdF již v nacistickém Německu a po roce 1945 pod jménem VW Brouk v SRN. Lze také jen těžko odolat pocitu, že Tatra 77 se později nenápadně nezrcadlí ve vynikajícím způsobem vylepšeném automobilu Citroen ID/DS série z šedesátých let, který, chcete-li, zdá se být poněkud Tatroidní či Tatroenoidní – alespoň dle názoru některých zapálených Tatra fundamentalistů.

Po zániku Rakousko-Uherského impéria (EU č. 1, jak je někdy nazýváno) byla Morava na mezinárodním poli reprezentována jen pomlčkou mezi Česko–Slovenskem a tichem mezi dvěma národními hymnami. Rozpad České a Slovenské federativní republiky v roce 1993 přinesl vznik nové – jen České republiky a nové přetrvávající ticho po výhradně jen české národní hymně získalo novou výpovědní hodnotu a stává se stále vyzývavějším.

* Výňatky z krátké eseje „Tisíciletí Tatry" © Vojta Dukát, 2002, doplněno 2013. Původní anglická verze byla v roce 2002 autorem poskytnuta k využití jako dodatky k textu z pera PhDr. Antonína Dufka o Vojtovi Dukátovi.

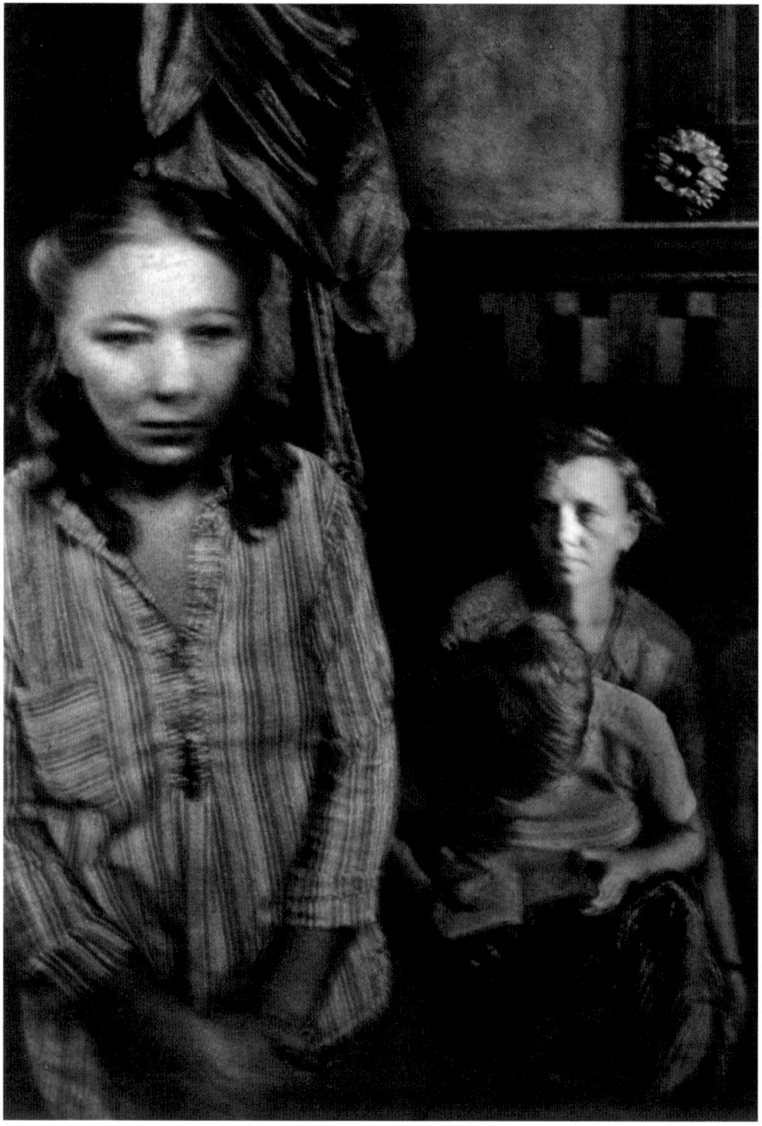

1 **Kalwaria Zebrzydowska, Poland / Polsko** 1986

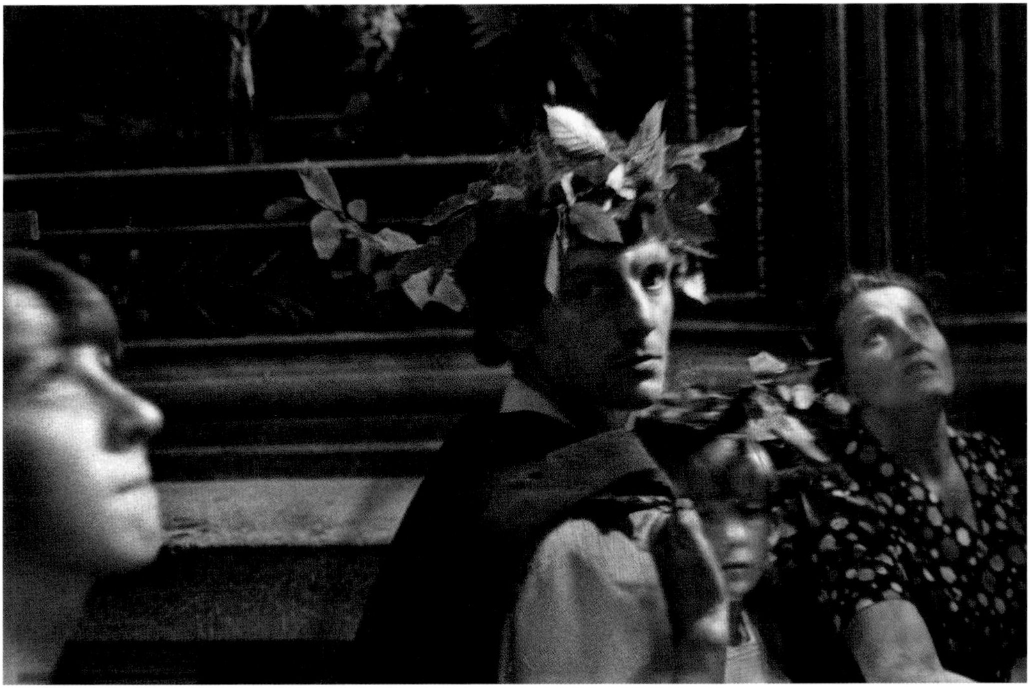

2 **Kalwaria Zebrzydowska, Poland / Polsko** 1982

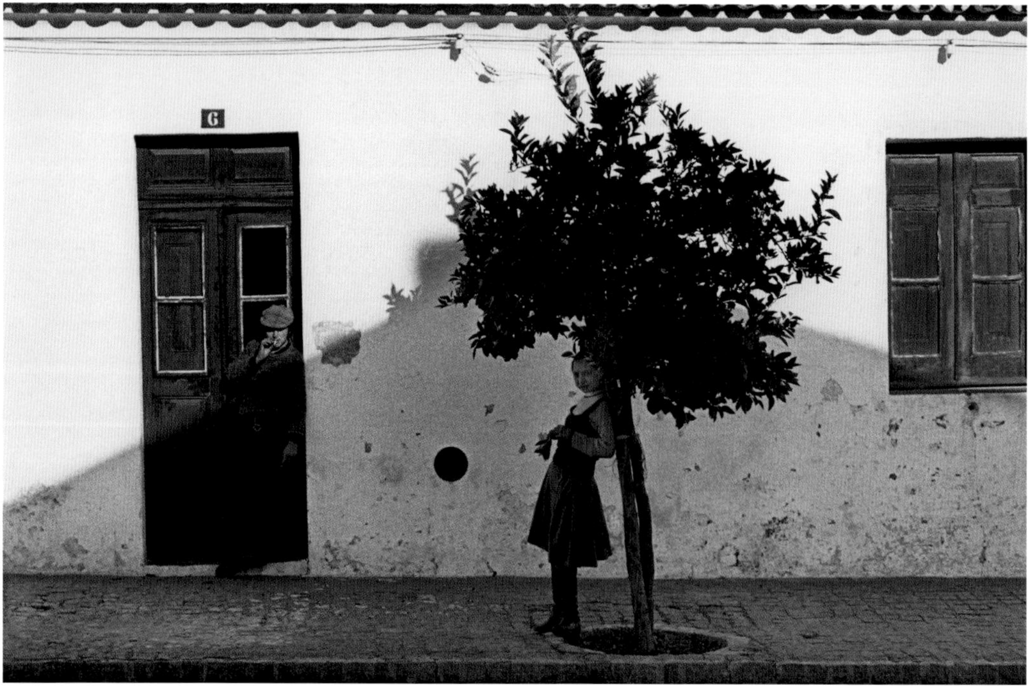

3 **Mourão, Portugal / Portugalsko** 1975

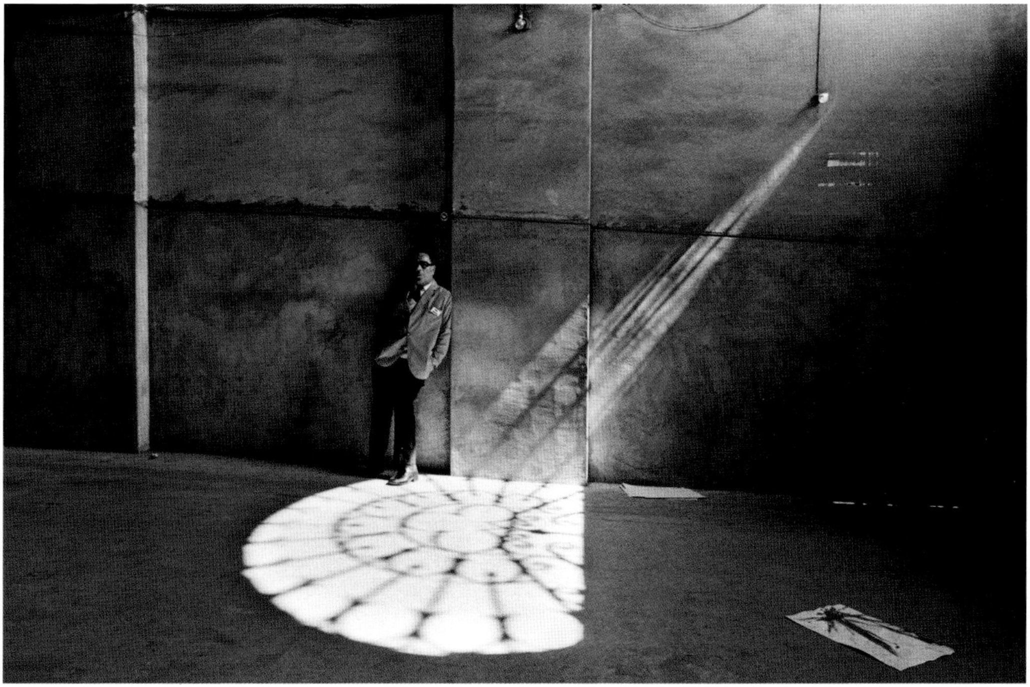

4 **Lisbon / Lisabon, Portugal / Portugalsko** 1975

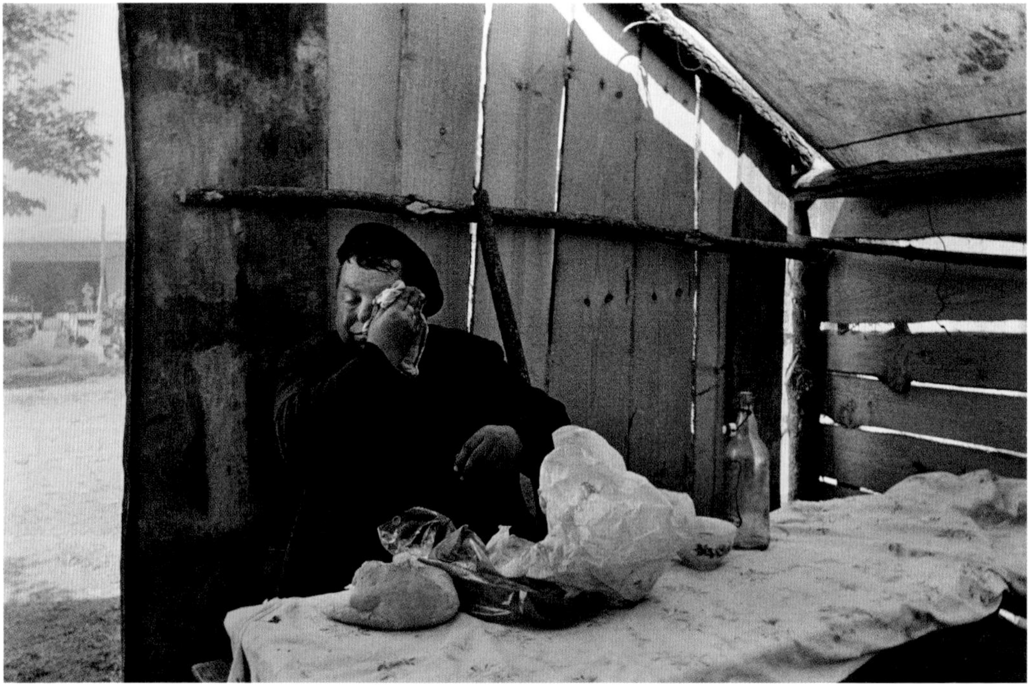

5 **Viana do Castelo, Portugal / Portugalsko** 1976

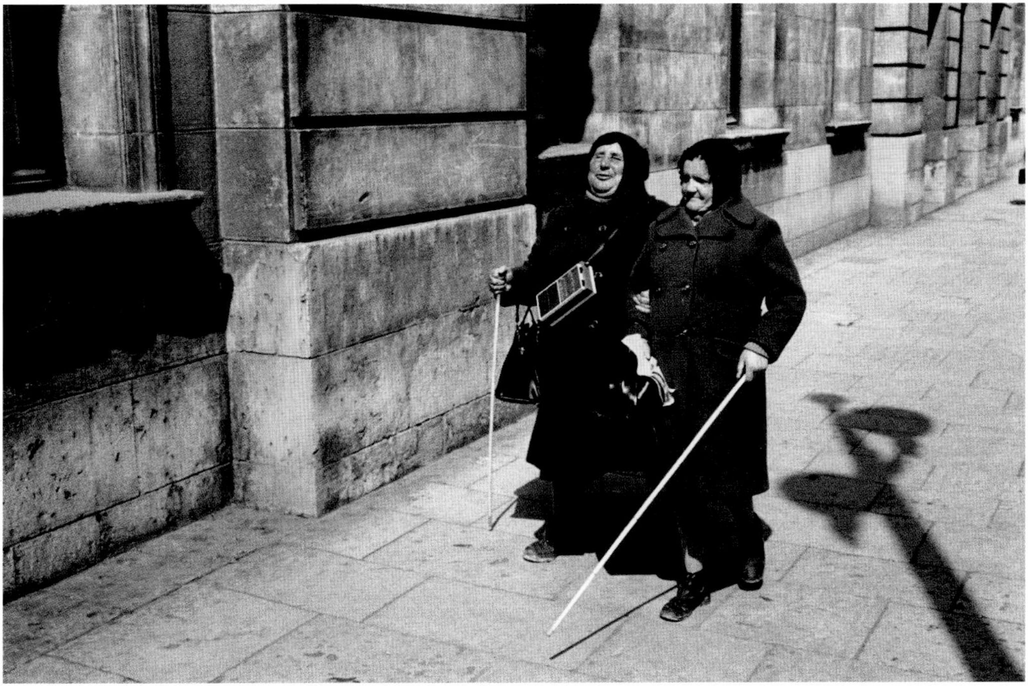

6 **Burgos, Spain / Španělsko** 1975

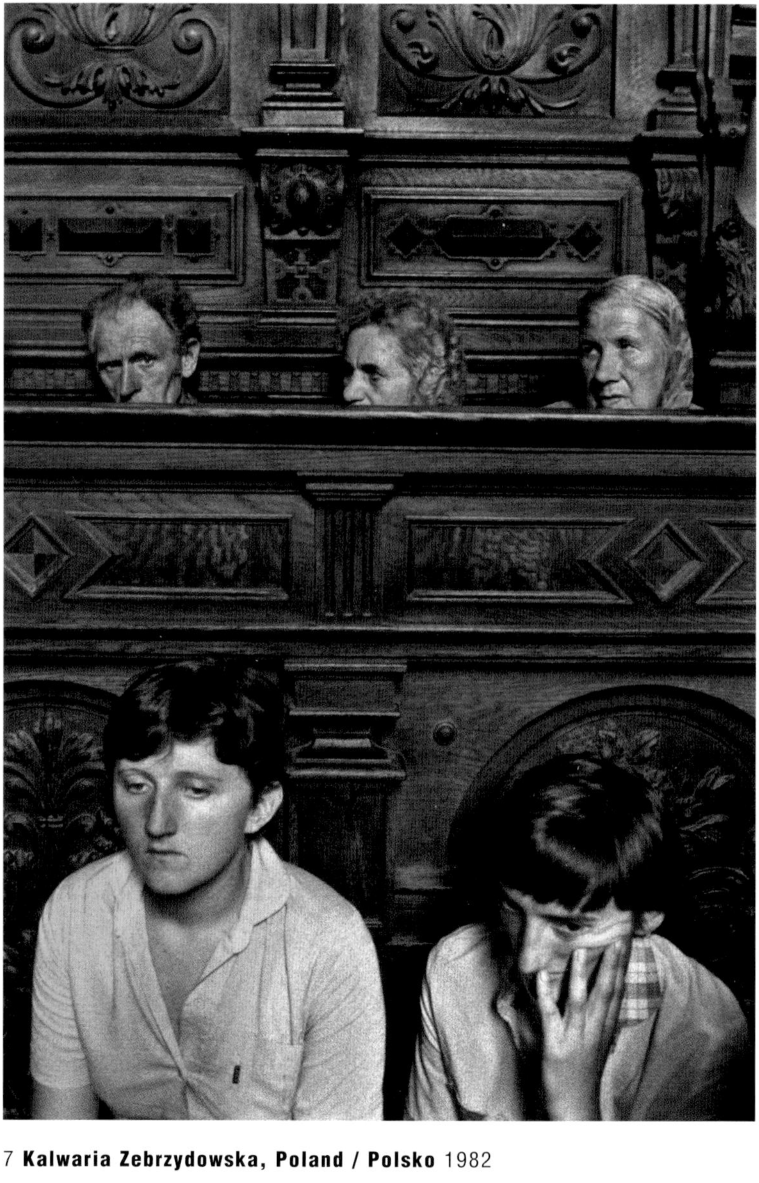

7 **Kalwaria Zebrzydowska, Poland / Polsko** 1982

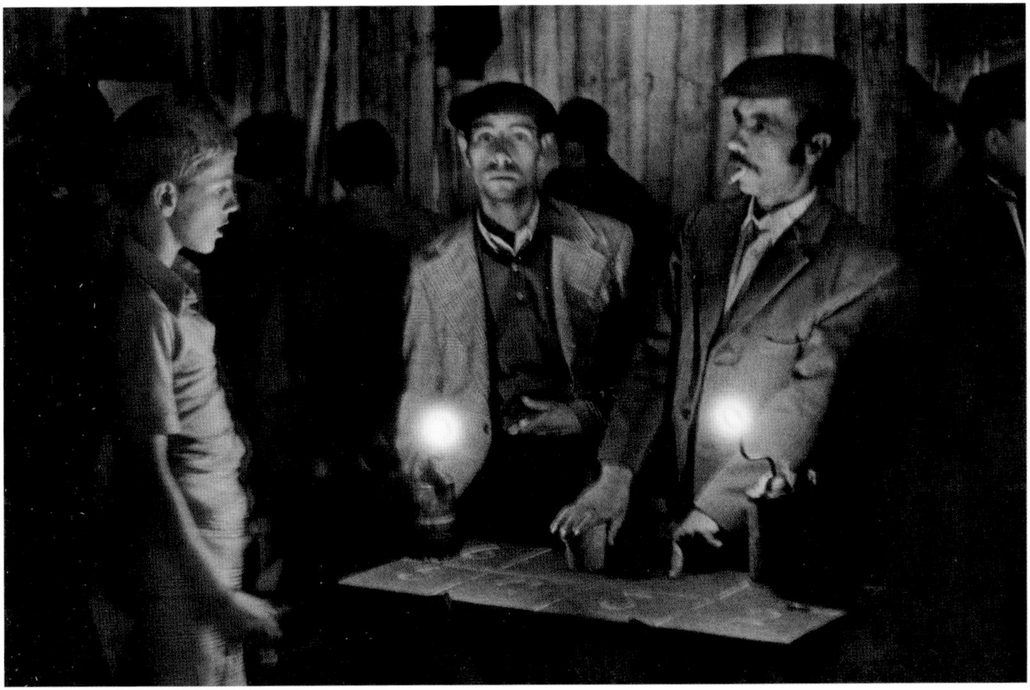

8 **Viana do Castelo, Portugal / Portugalsko** 1976

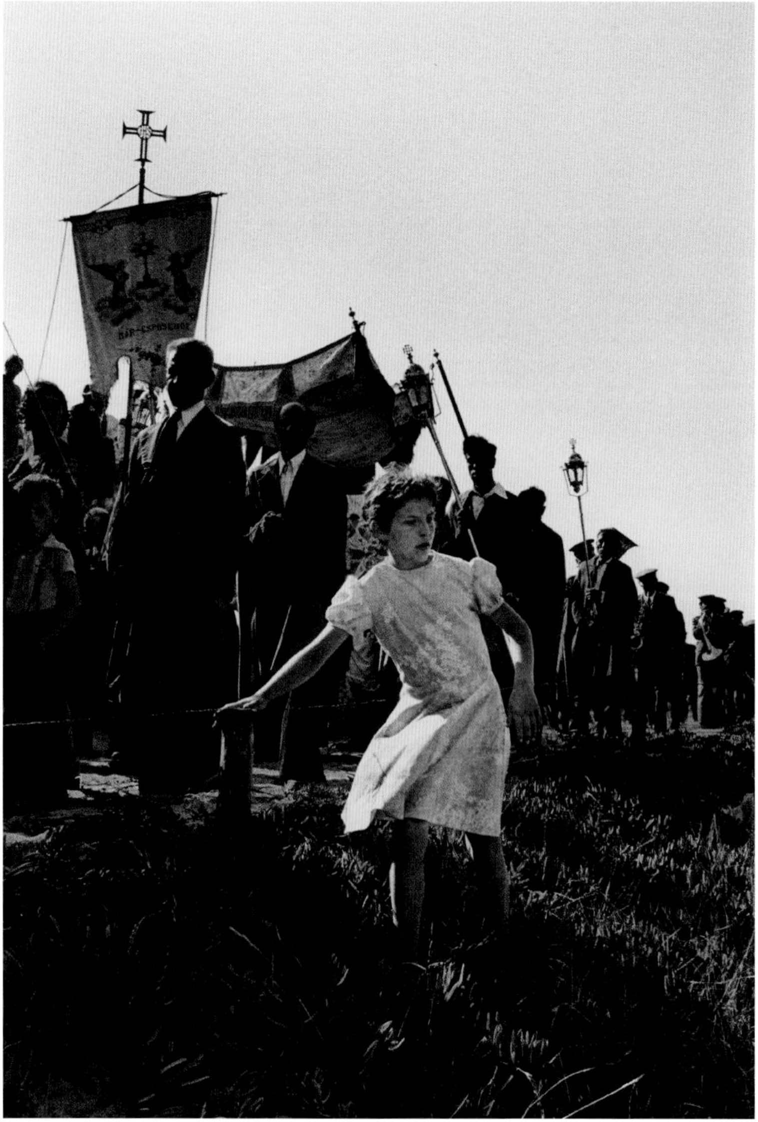

9 **São Bartolomeu-do-Mar, Esposende, Portugal / Portugalsko** 1977

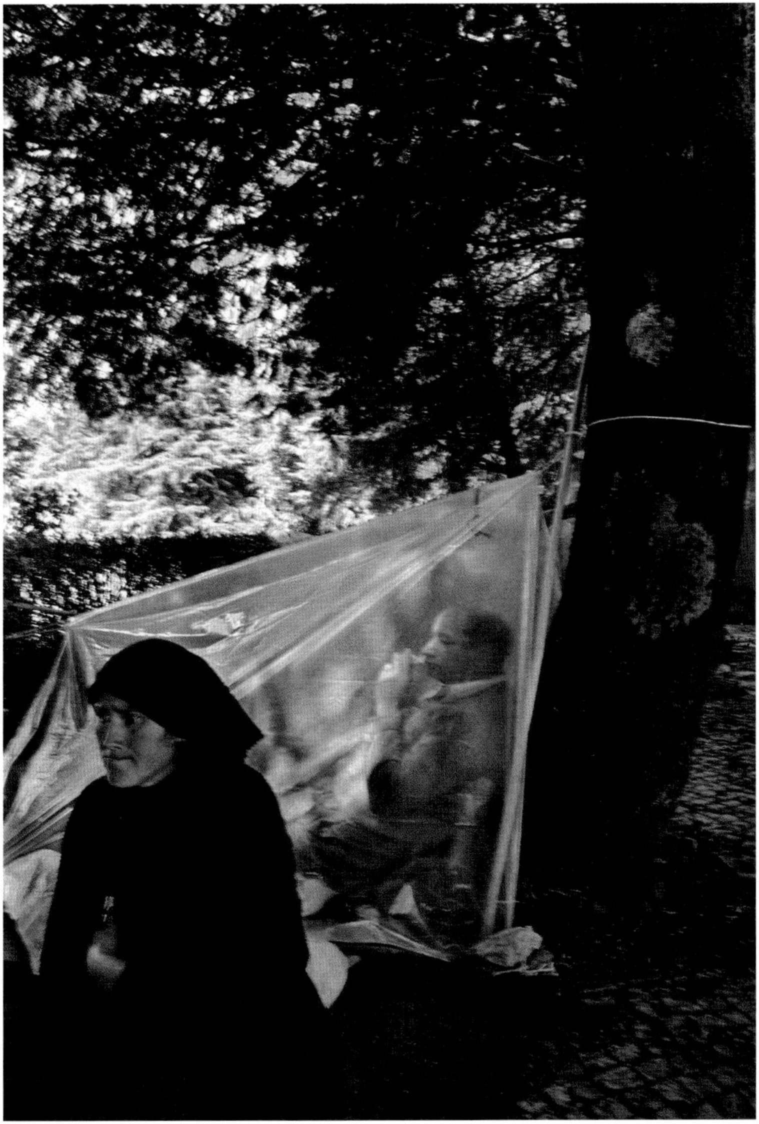

10 **Fátima, Portugal / Portugalsko** 1978

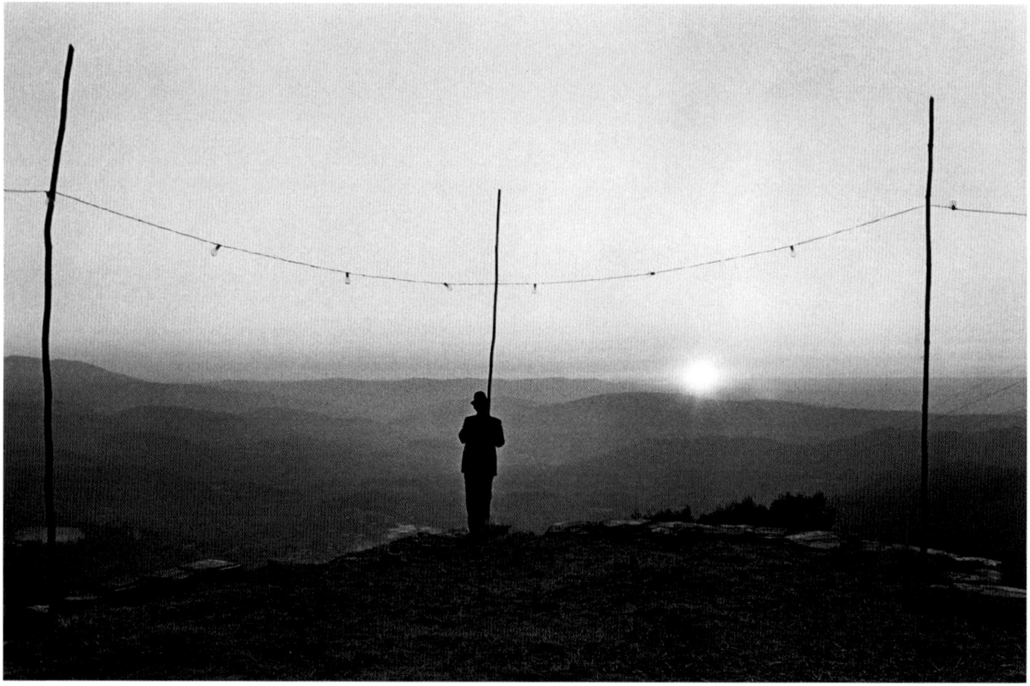

11 **Nossa Senhora da Mó, Portugal / Portugalsko** 1979

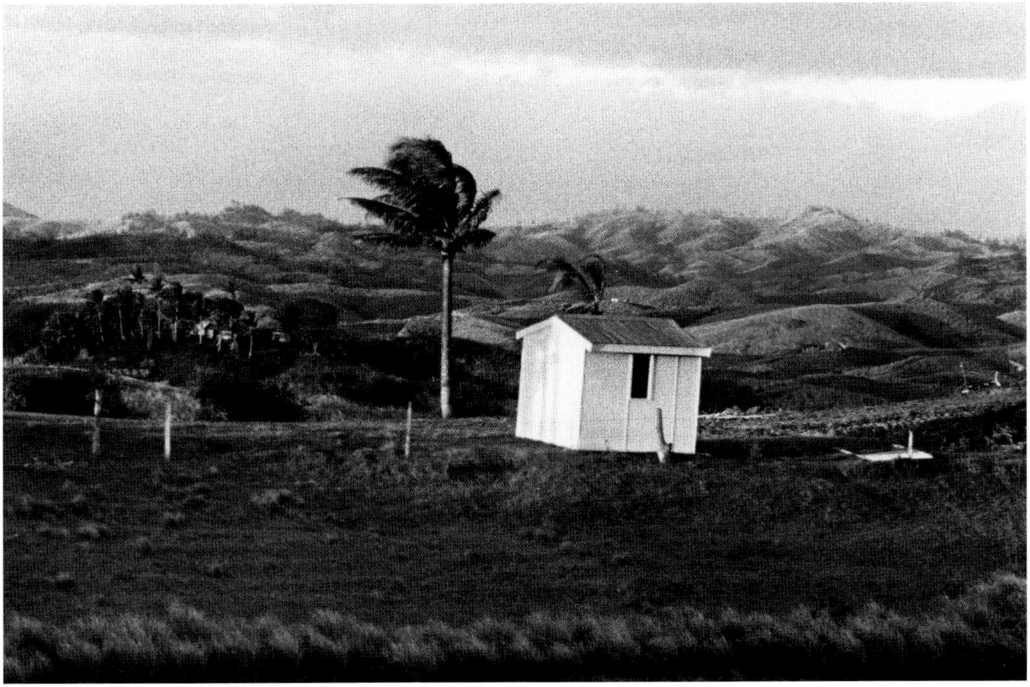

12 **Fiji / Ostrovy Fidži** 1973

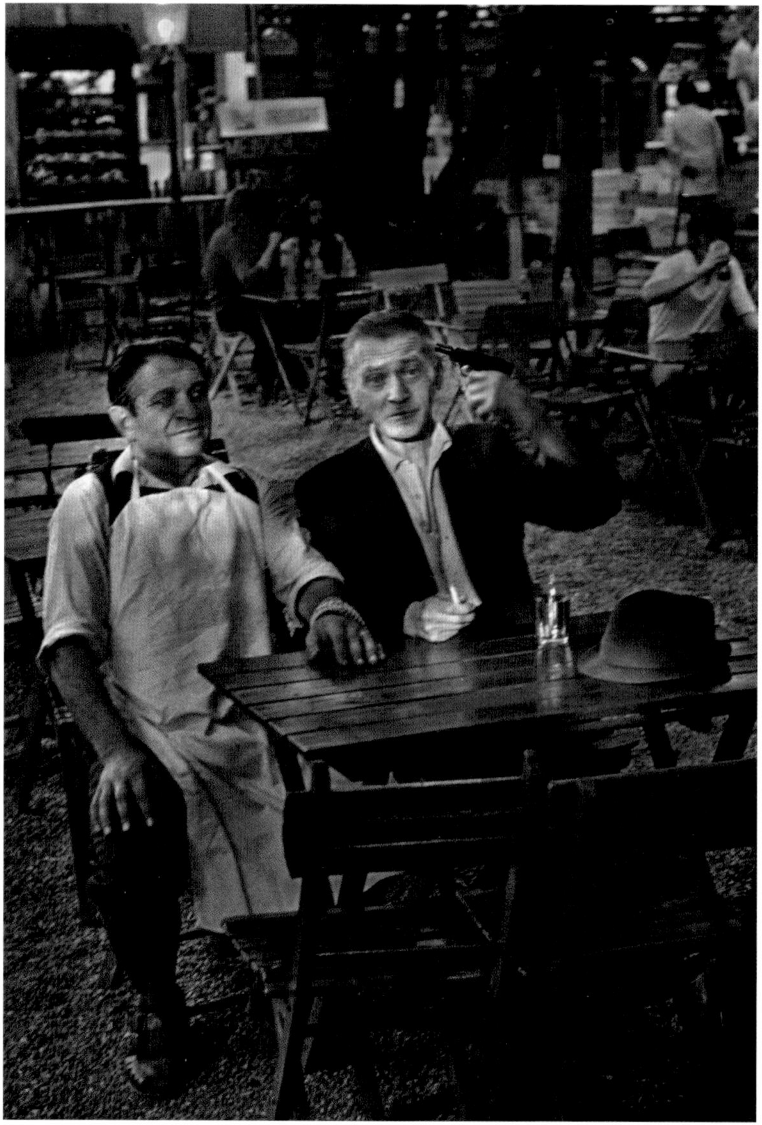

13 **Vienna / Vídeň, Austria / Rakousko** 1977

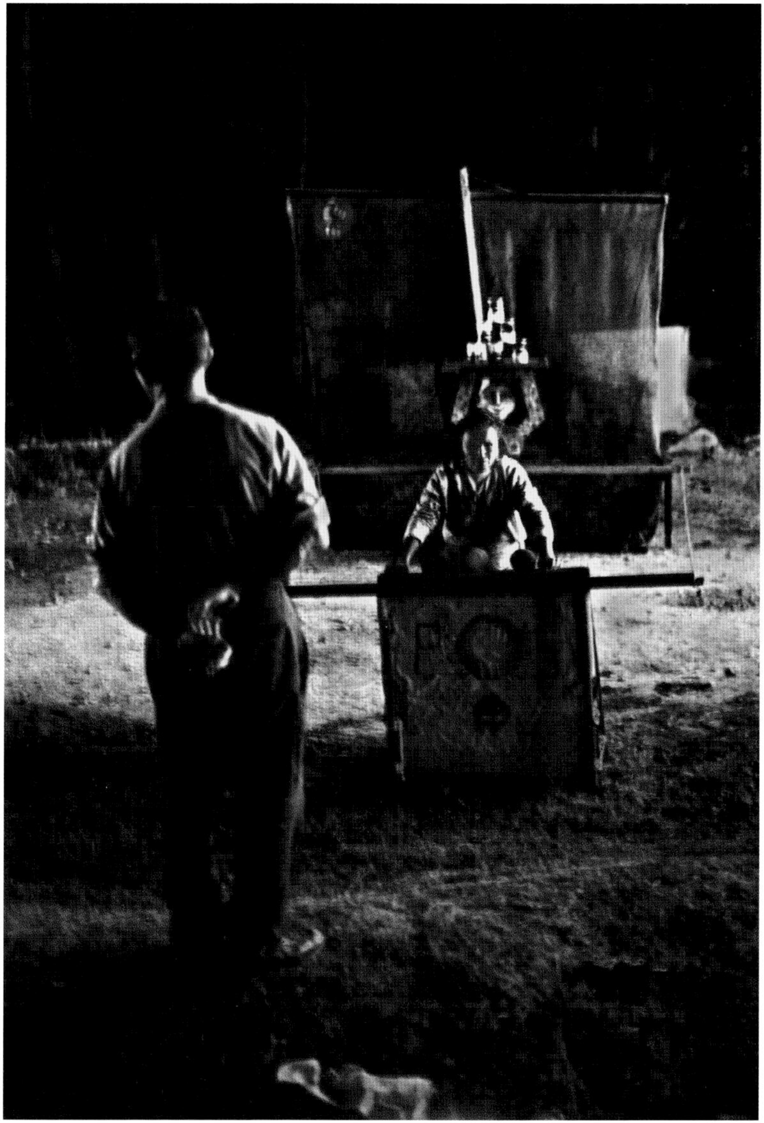

14 **Viana do Castelo, Portugal / Portugalsko** 1977

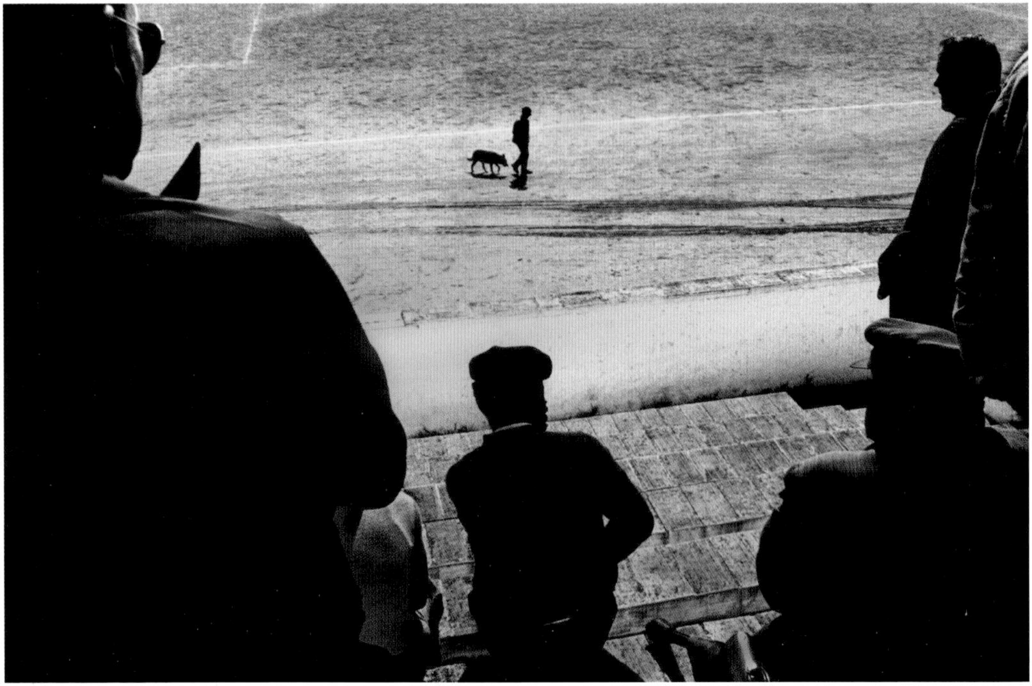

15 **Beja, Portugal / Portugalsko** 1975

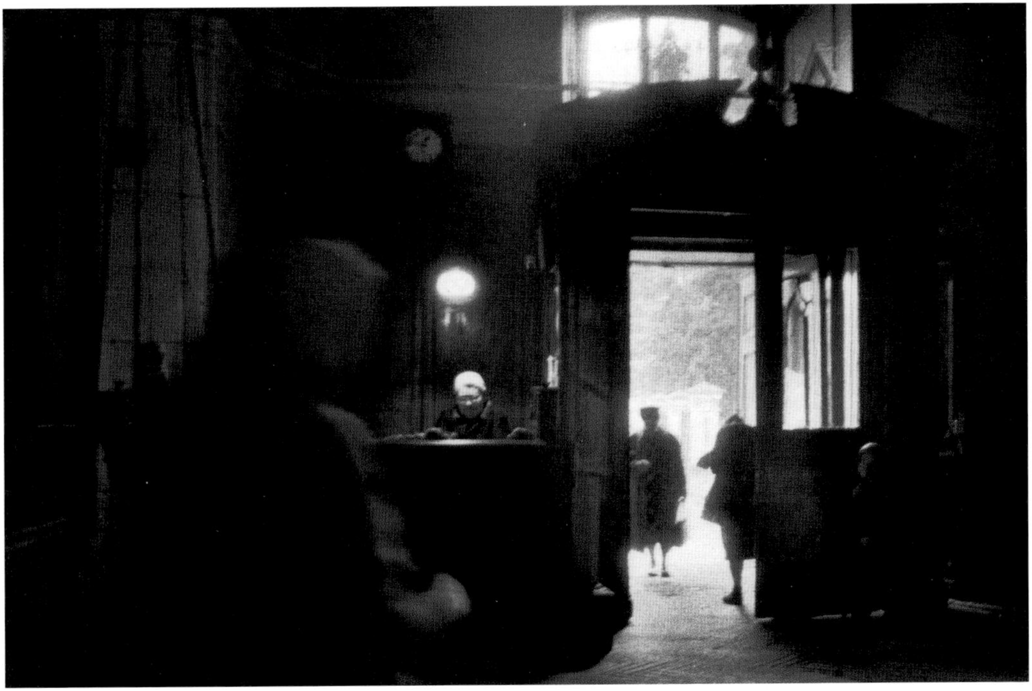

16 **Leningrad, USSR / Sovětský svaz** 1985

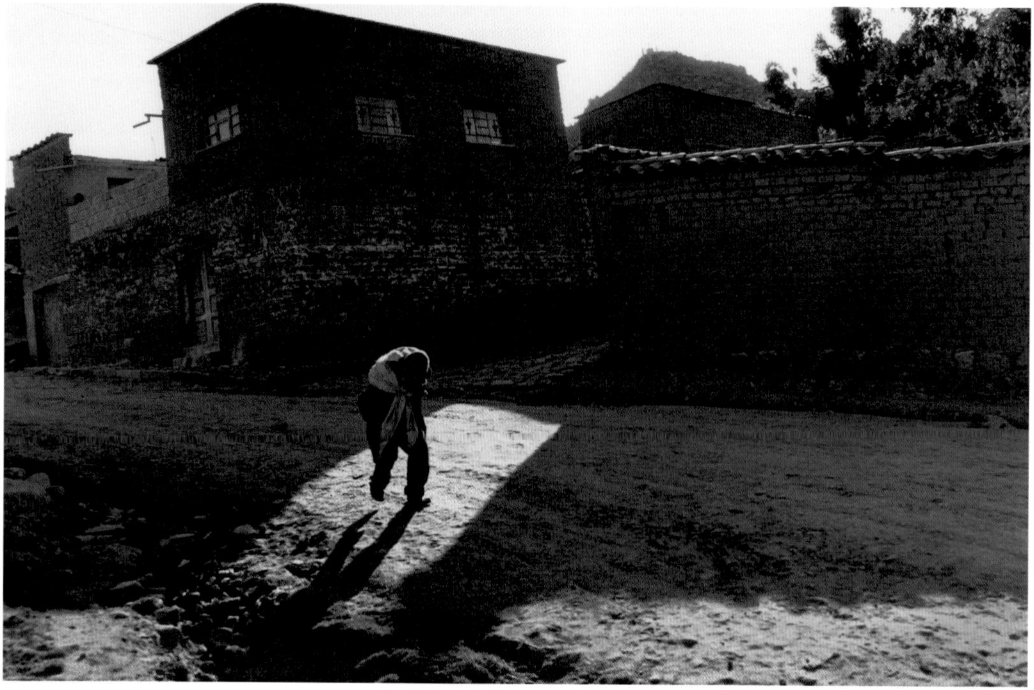

17 **Copacabana, Lake Titicaca / Copacabana, Jezero Titicaca, Bolivia / Bolívie** 1983

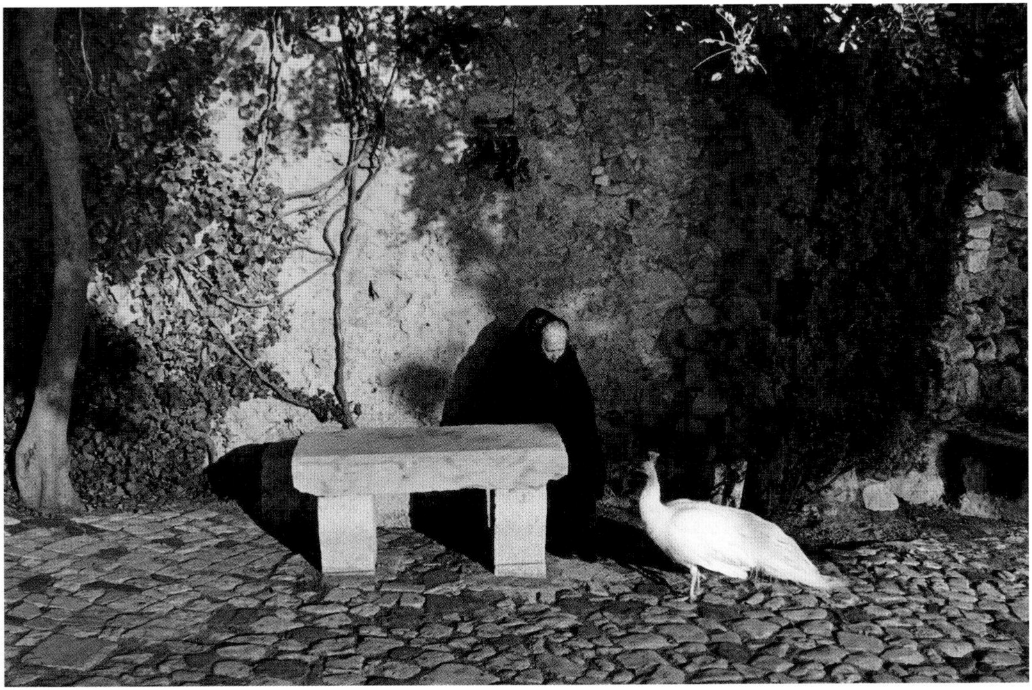

18 **Lisbon / Lisabon, Portugal / Portugalsko** 1979

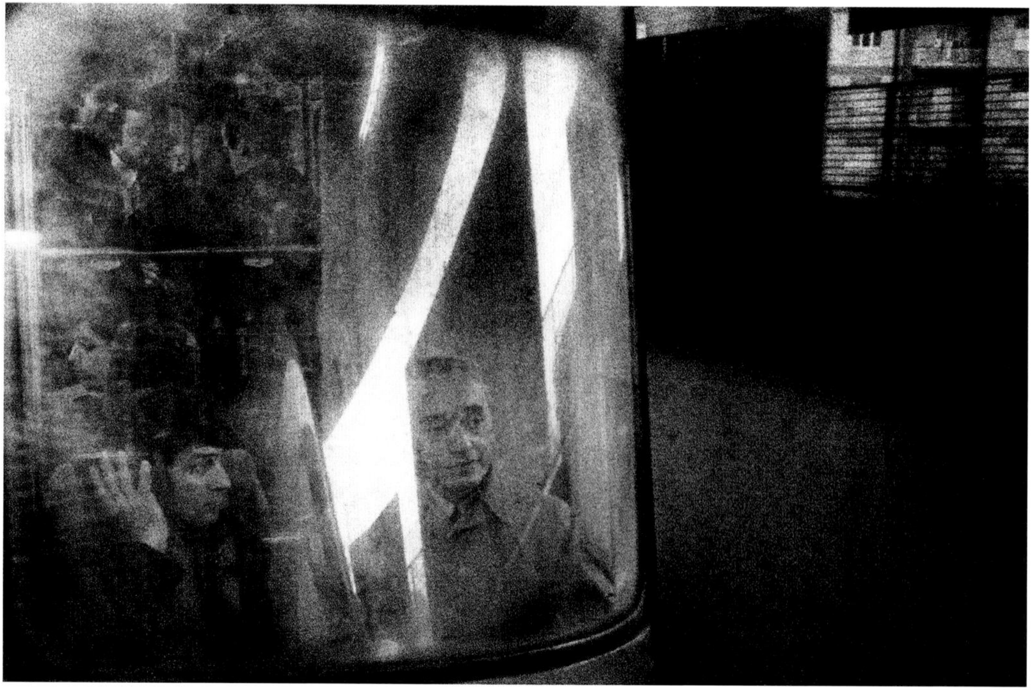

19 **Rome / Řím, Italy / Itálie** 1972

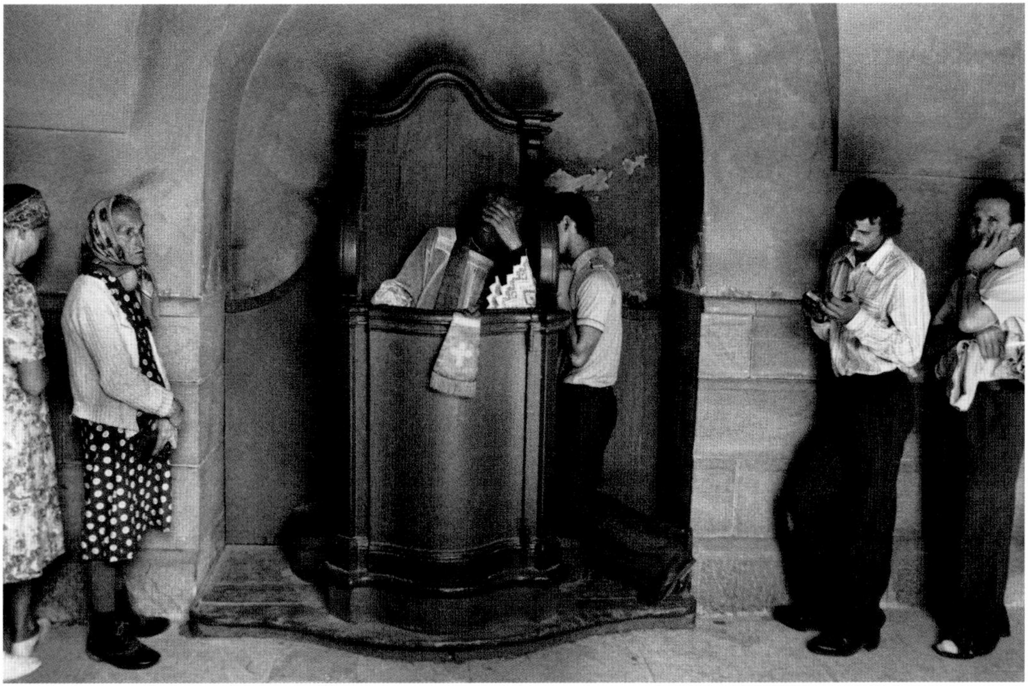

20 **Kalwaria Zebrzydowska, Poland / Polsko** 1986

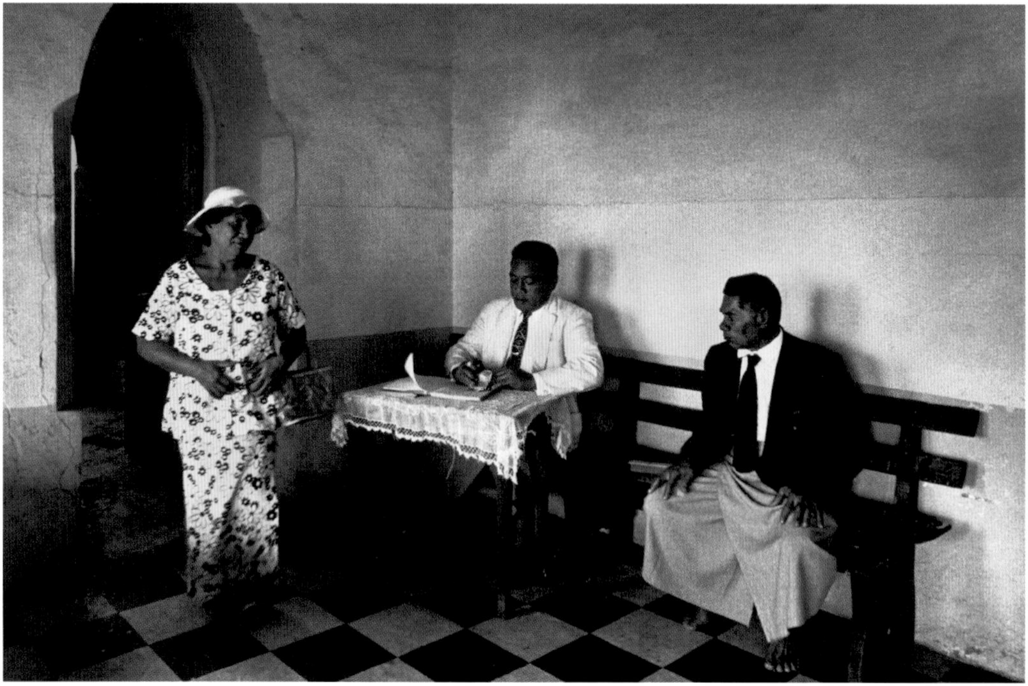

21 **Western Samoa / Západní Samoa** 1973

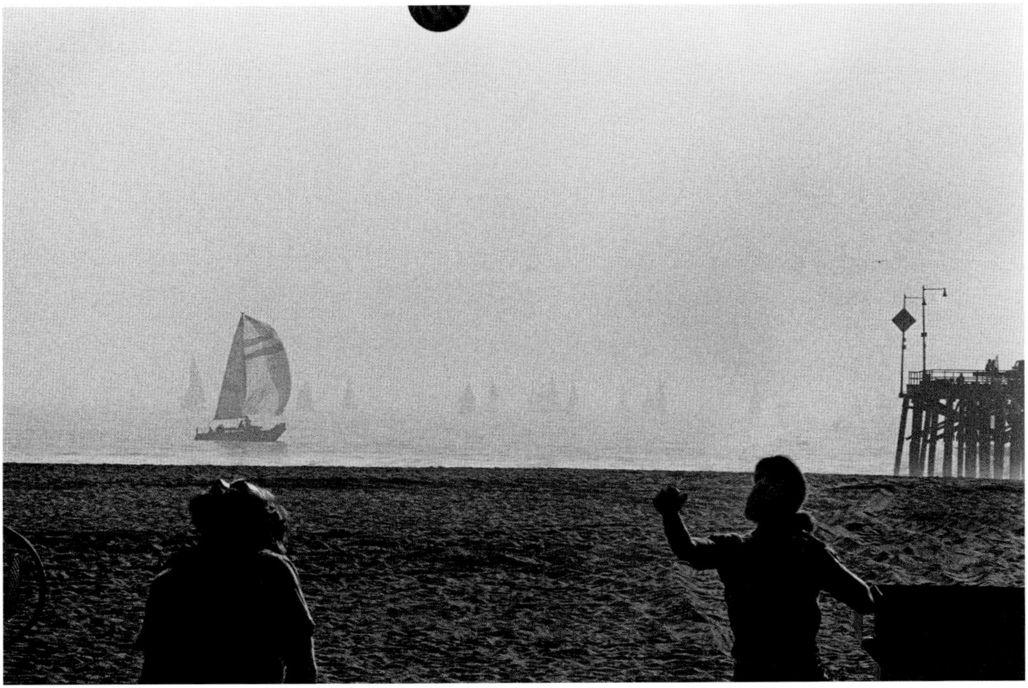

22 **California / Kalifornie, USA** 1973

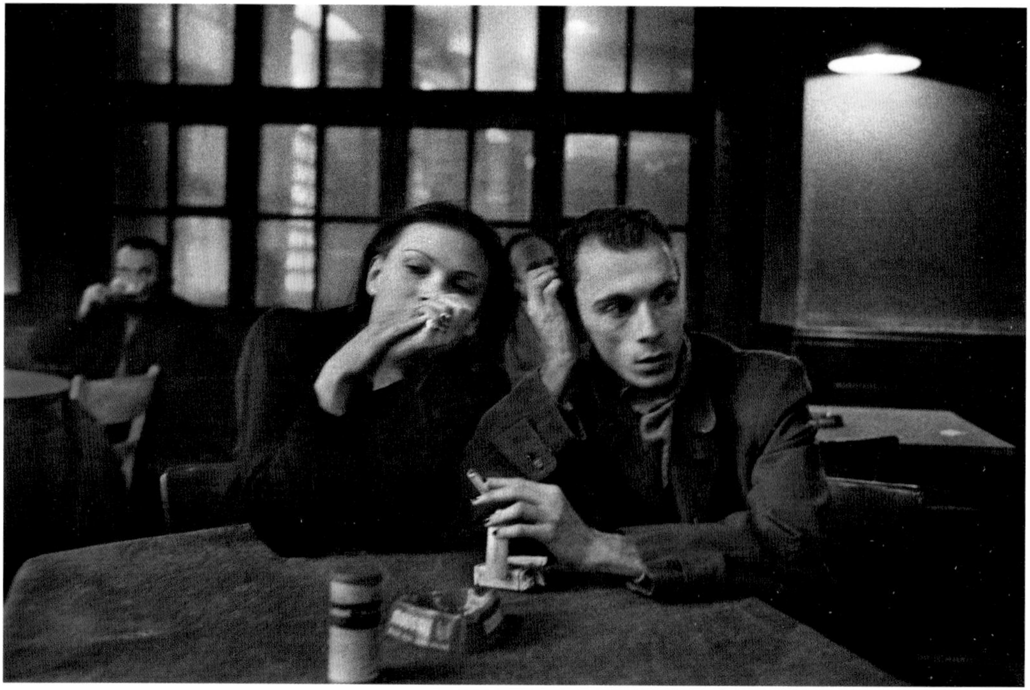

23 **Zurich / Curych, Switzerland / Švýcarsko** 1979

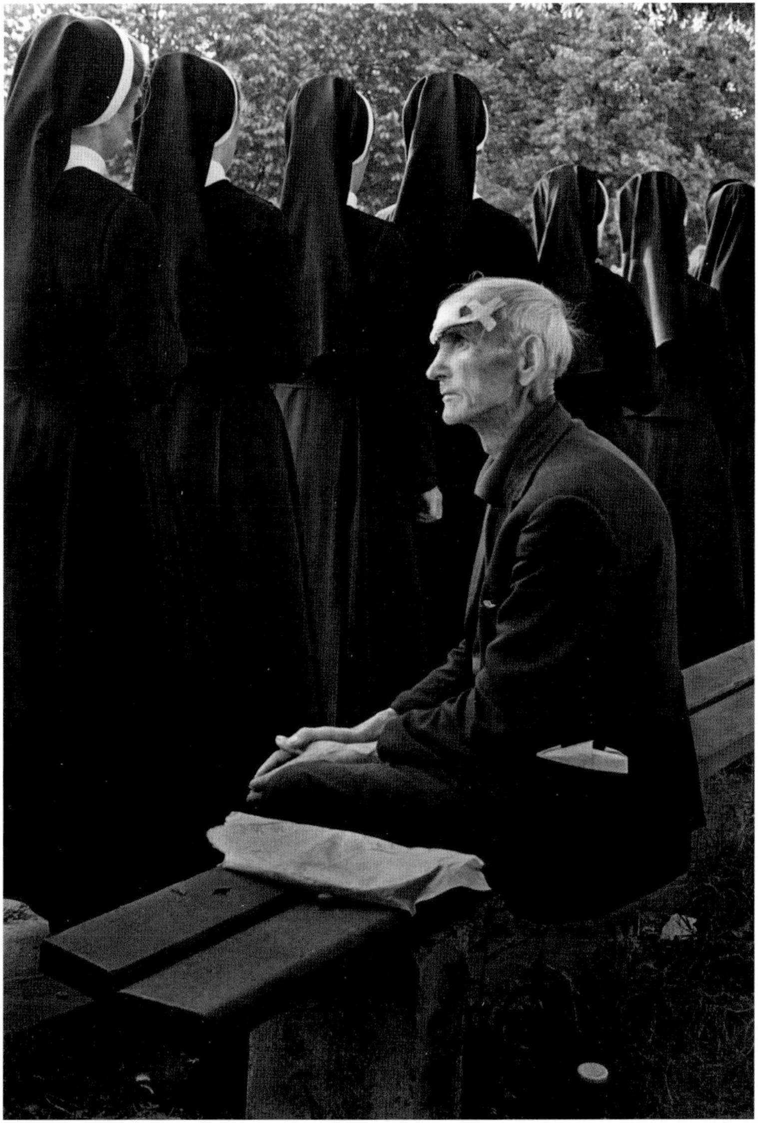

24 **Częstochowa, Poland / Polsko** 1986

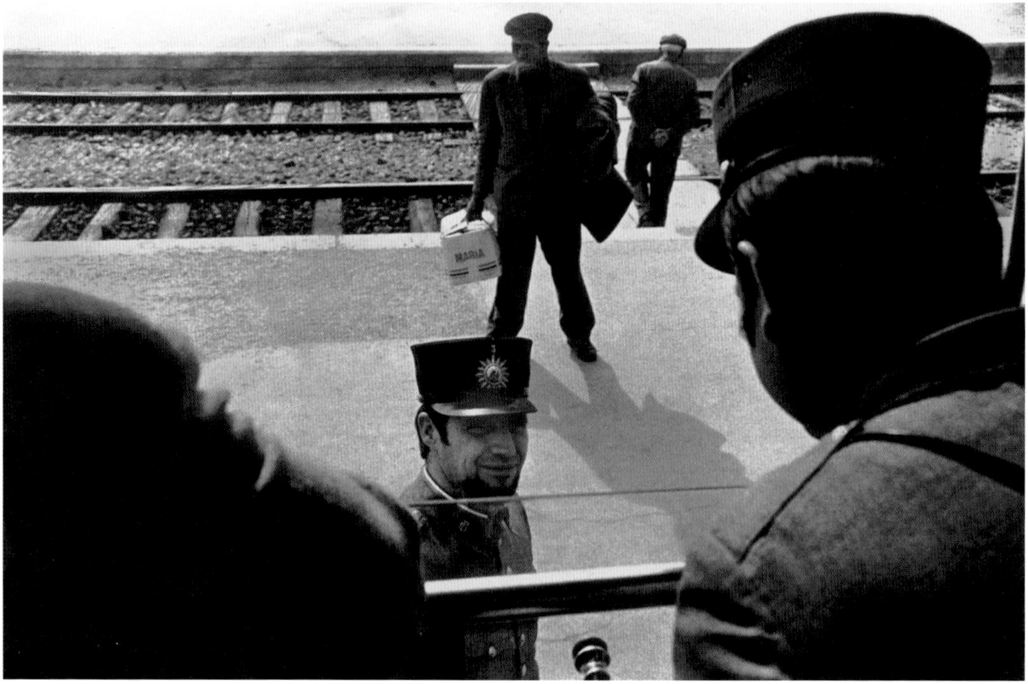

25 **Vilar-Formoso, Portugal / Portugalsko** 1975

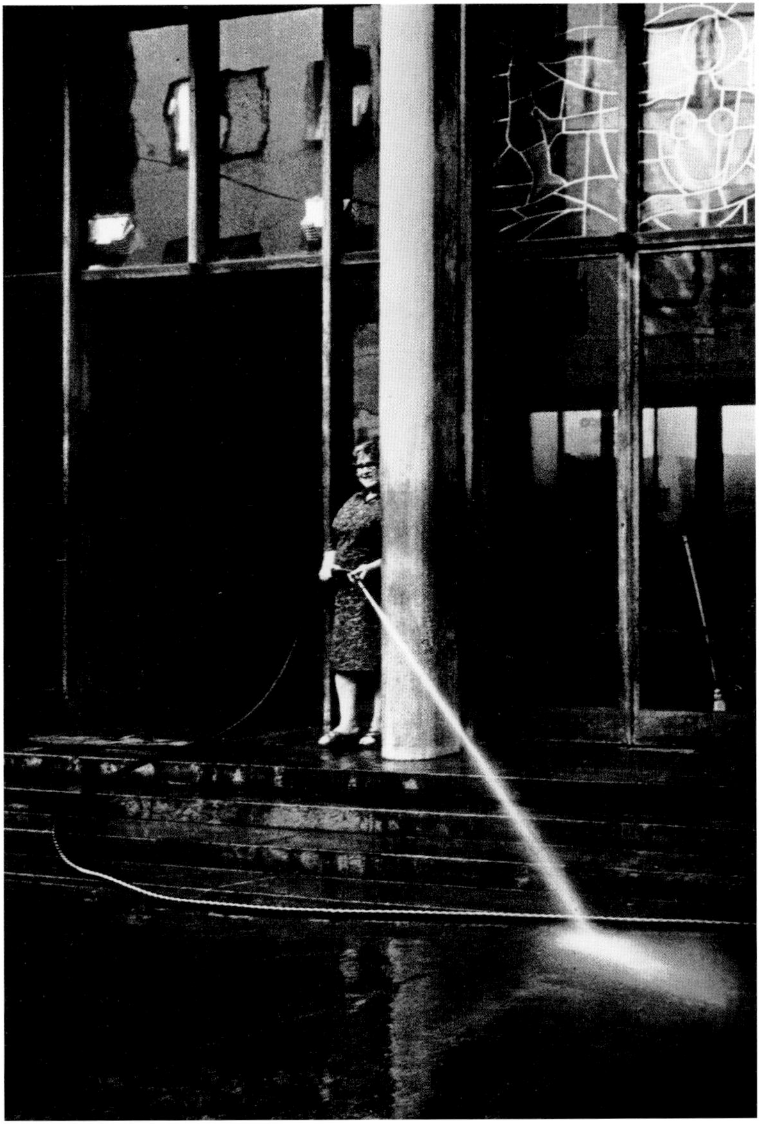

26 **Basel / Basilej, Switzerland / Švýcarsko** 1979

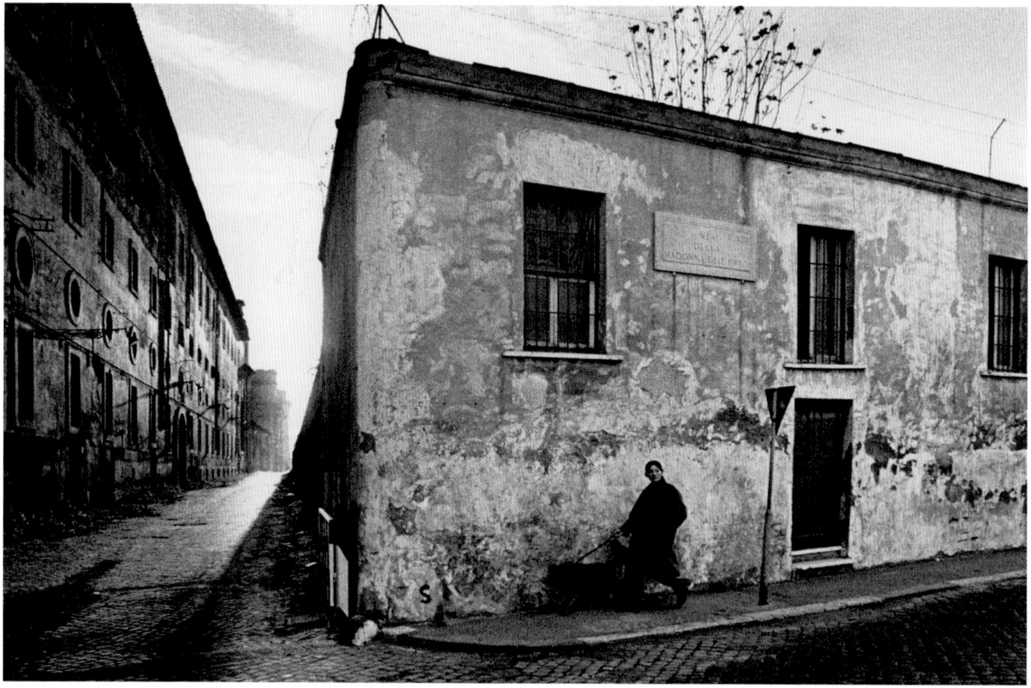

27 **Rome / Řím, Italy / Itálie** 1972

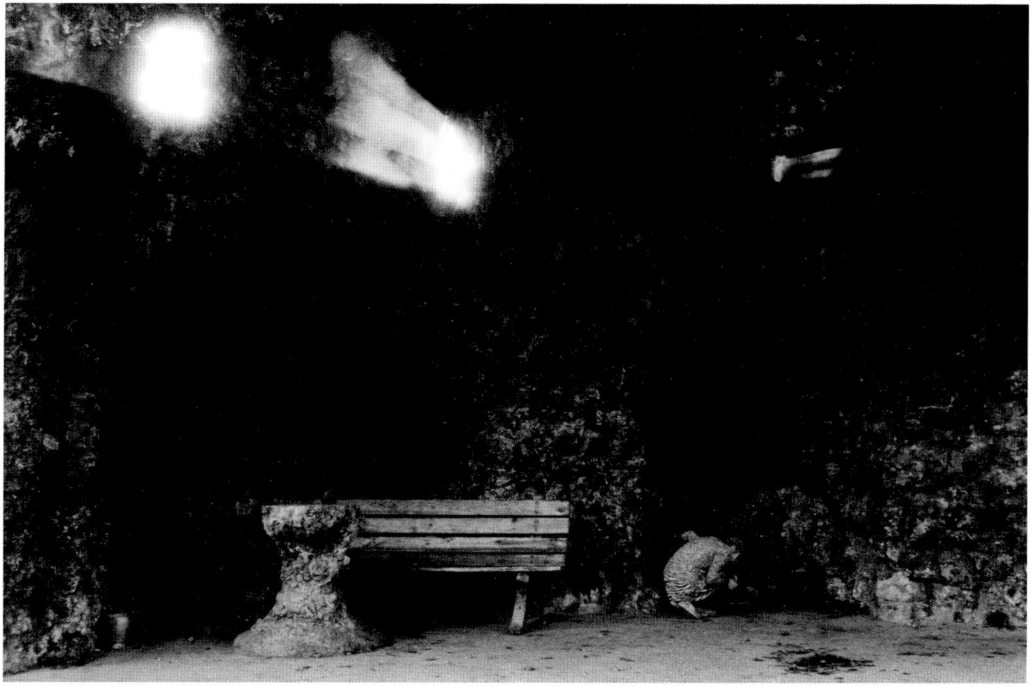

28 **Łódź, Poland / Polsko** 1988

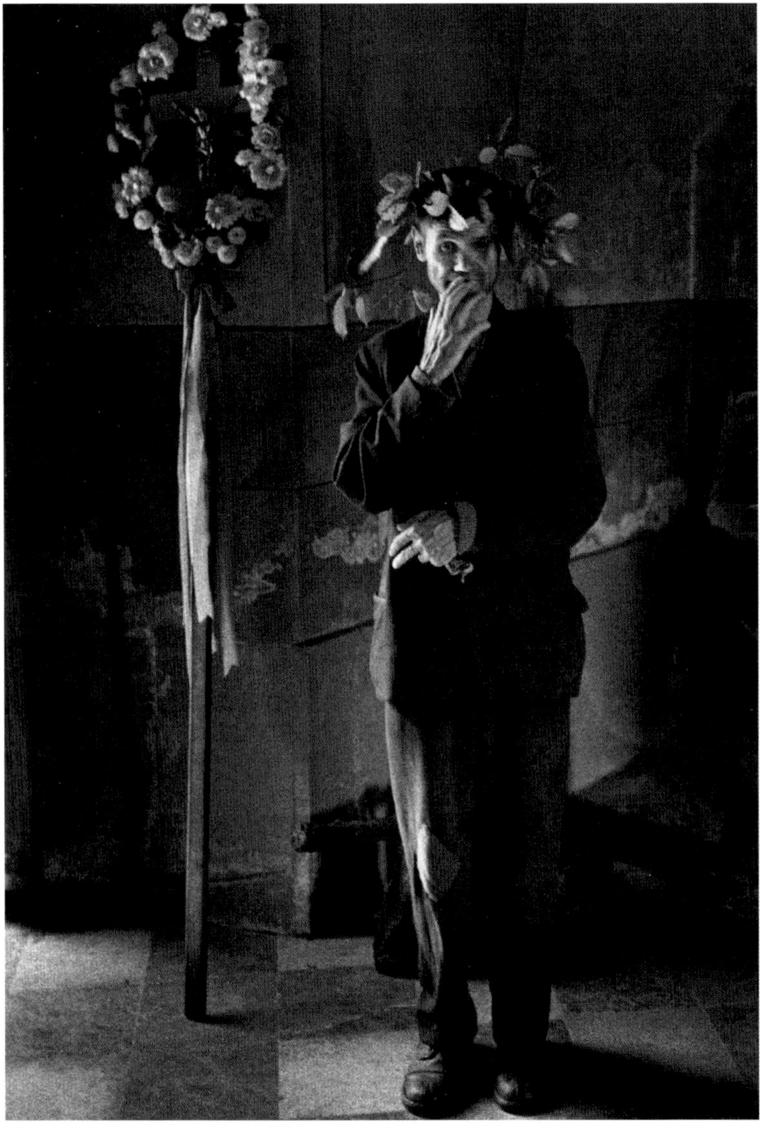

29 **Kalwaria Zebrzydowska, Poland / Polsko** 1982

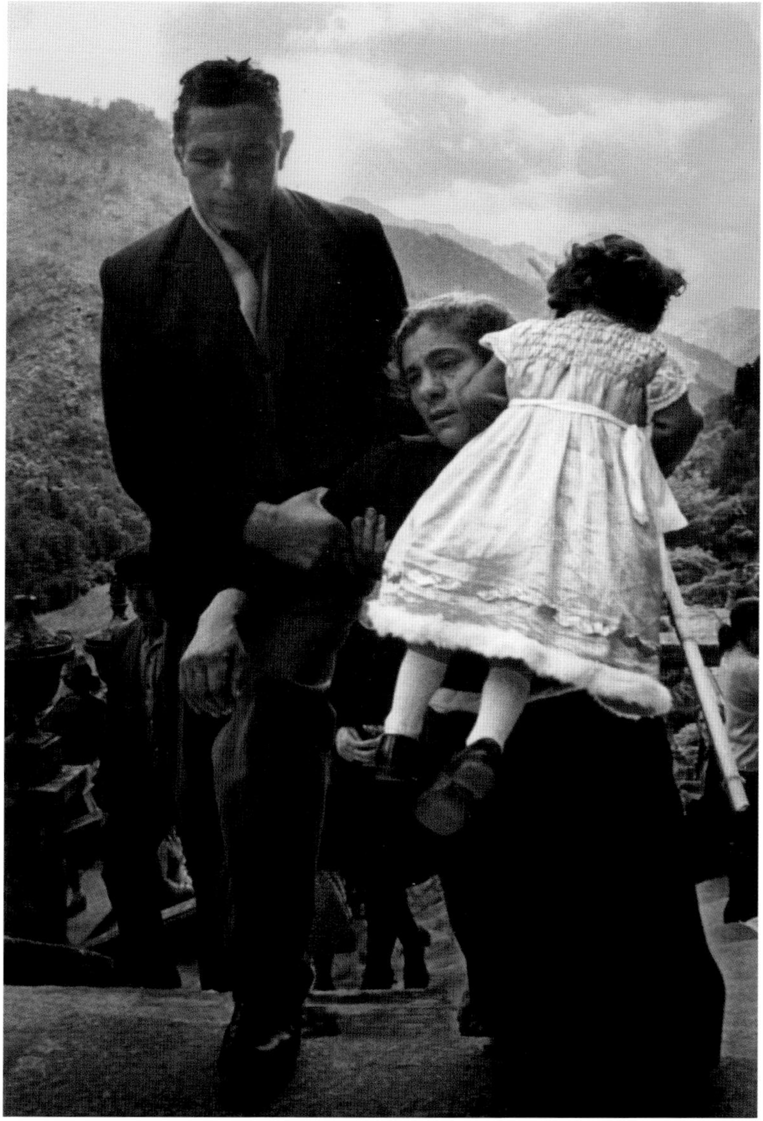

30 **Portugal / Portugalsko** 1977

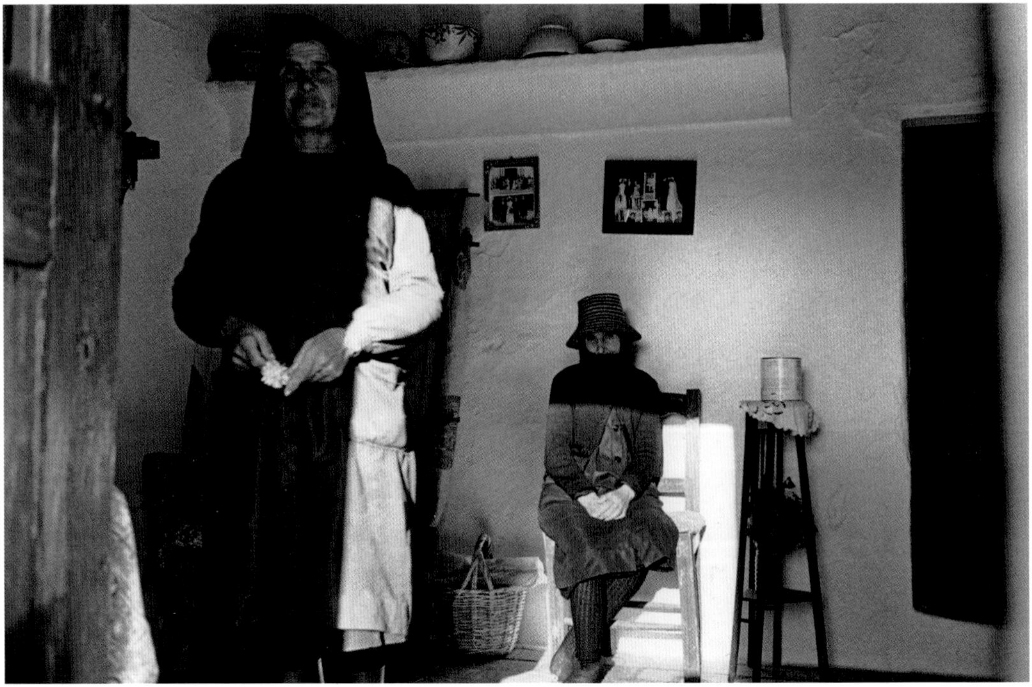

31 **Portugal / Portugalsko** 1976

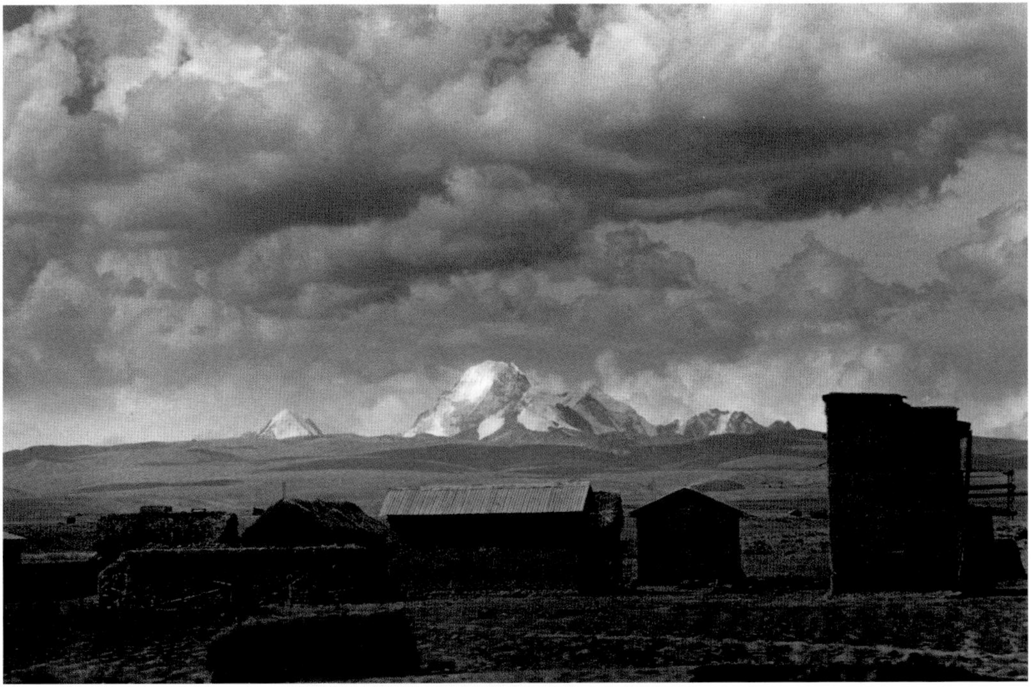

32 **Near La Paz / Poblíž La Pazu, Bolivia / Bolívie** 1983

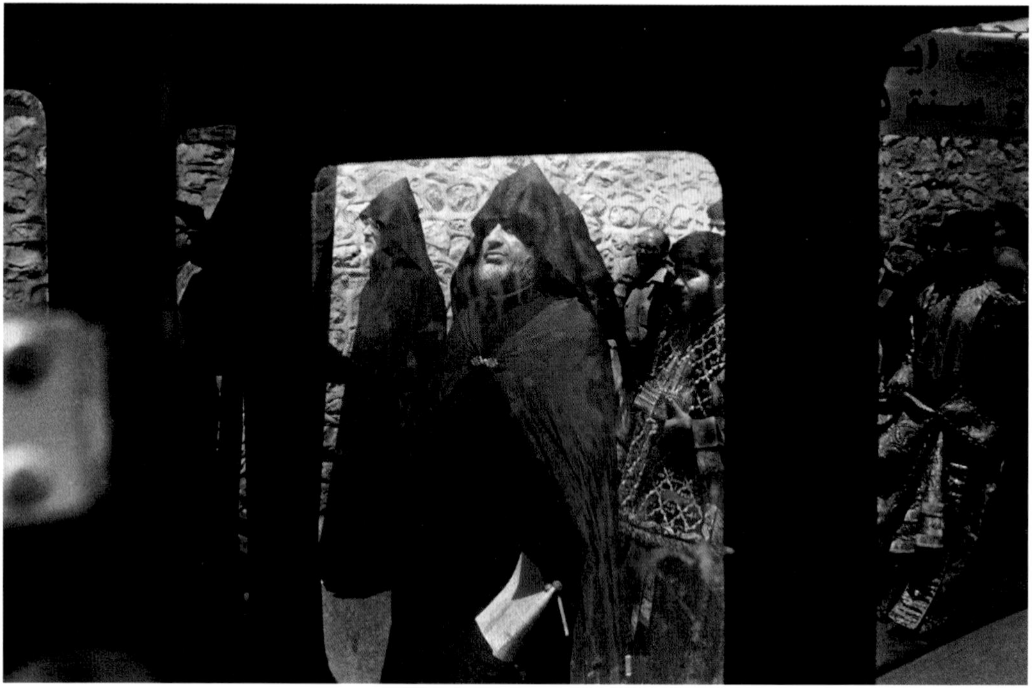

33 **Jerusalem / Jeruzalém, Israel / Izrael** 1986

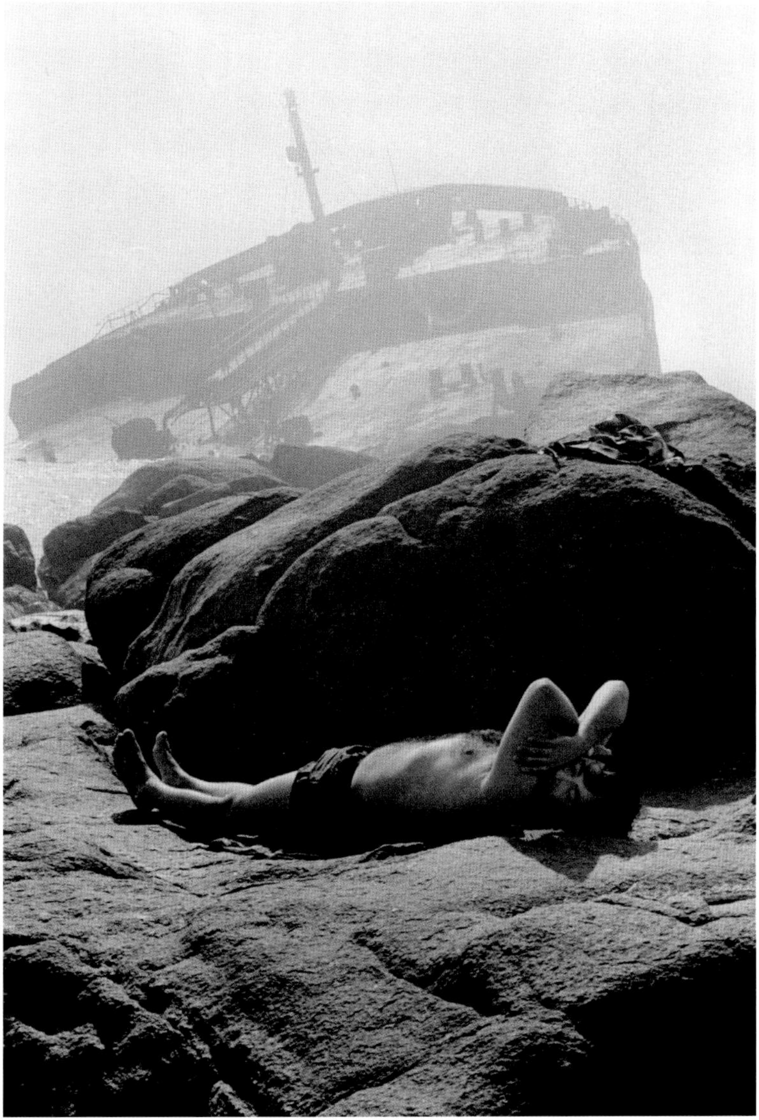

34 **Porto, Portugal / Portugalsko** 1977

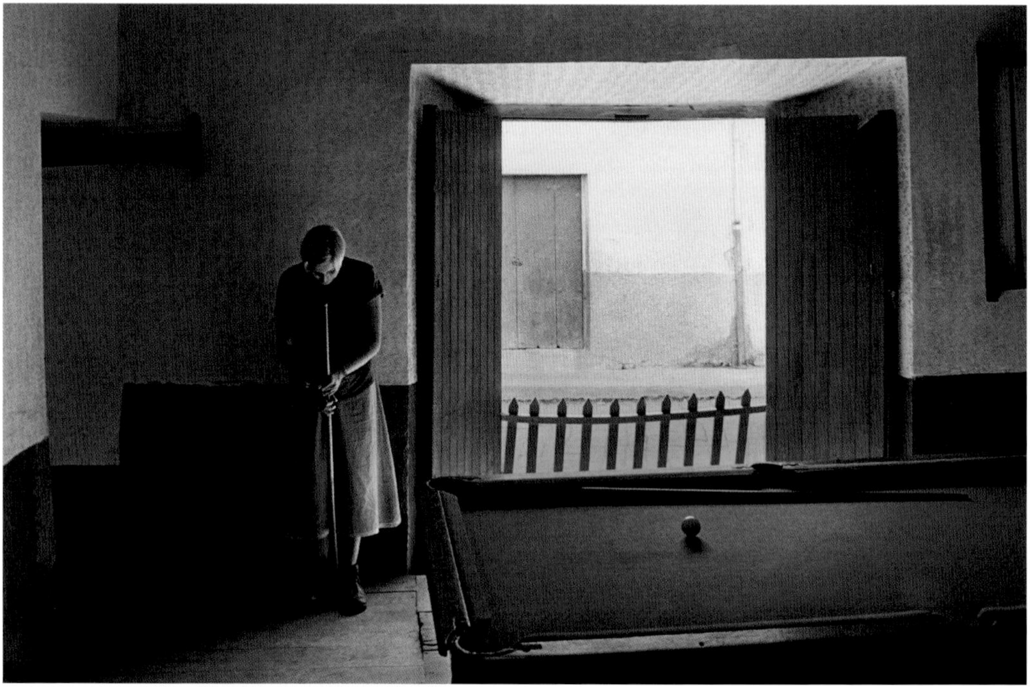

35 **Coroico, Bolivia / Bolívie** 1983

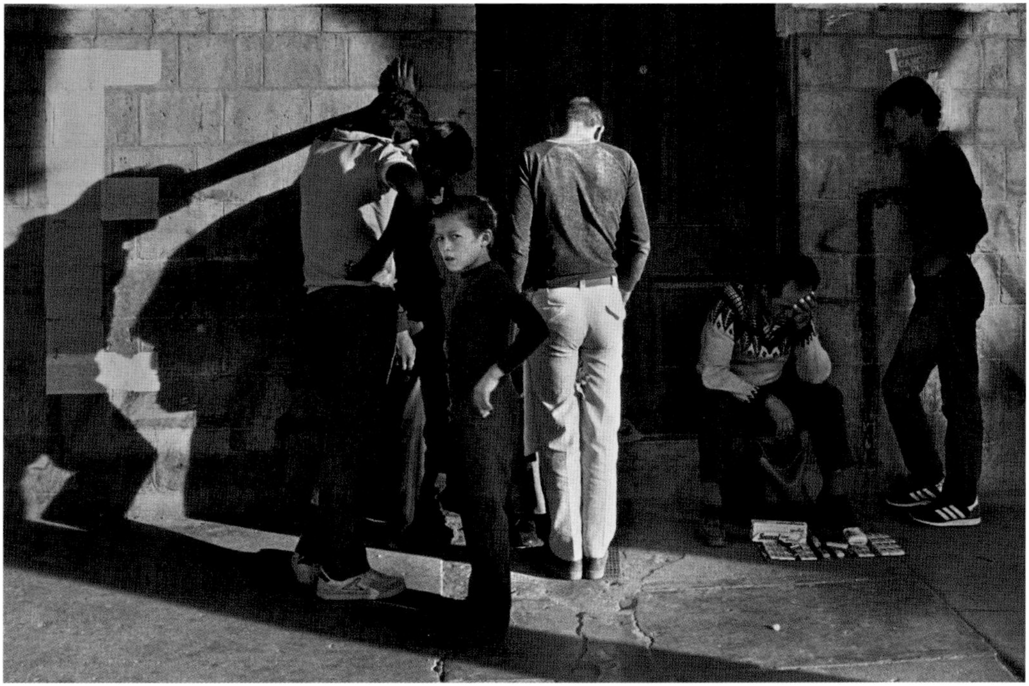

36 **Cochabamba, Bolivia / Bolívie** 1983

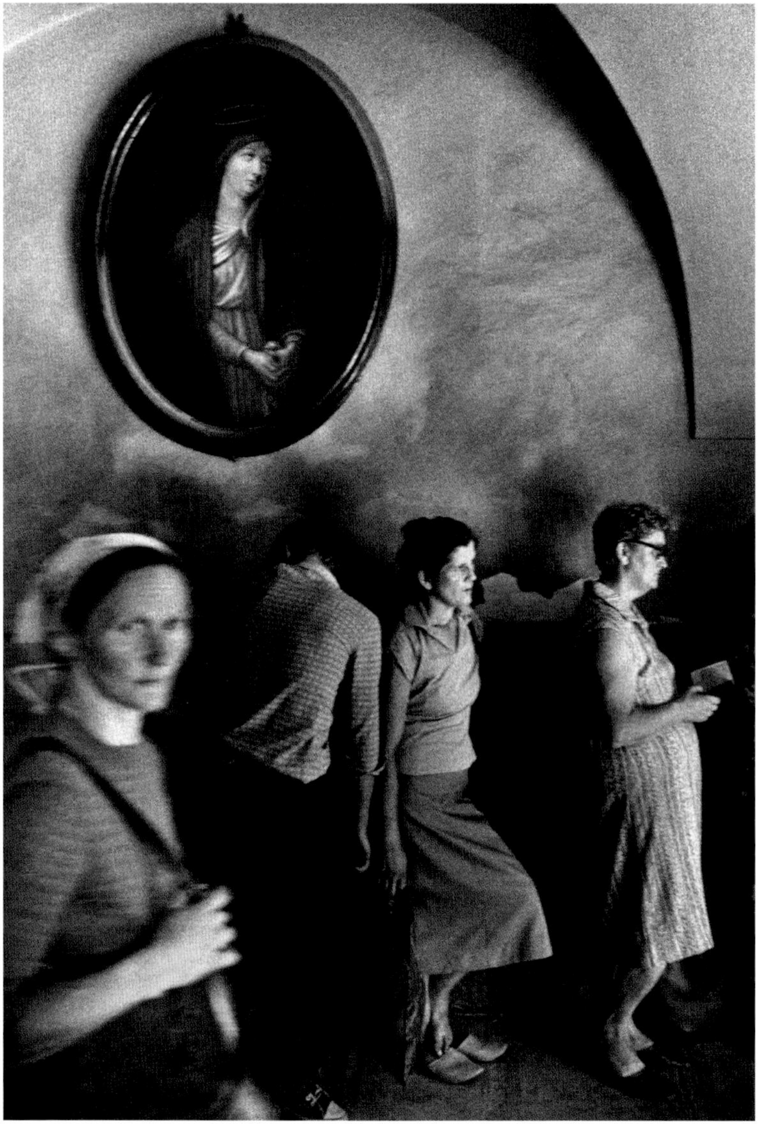

37 **Kalwaria Zebrzydowska, Poland / Polsko** 1986

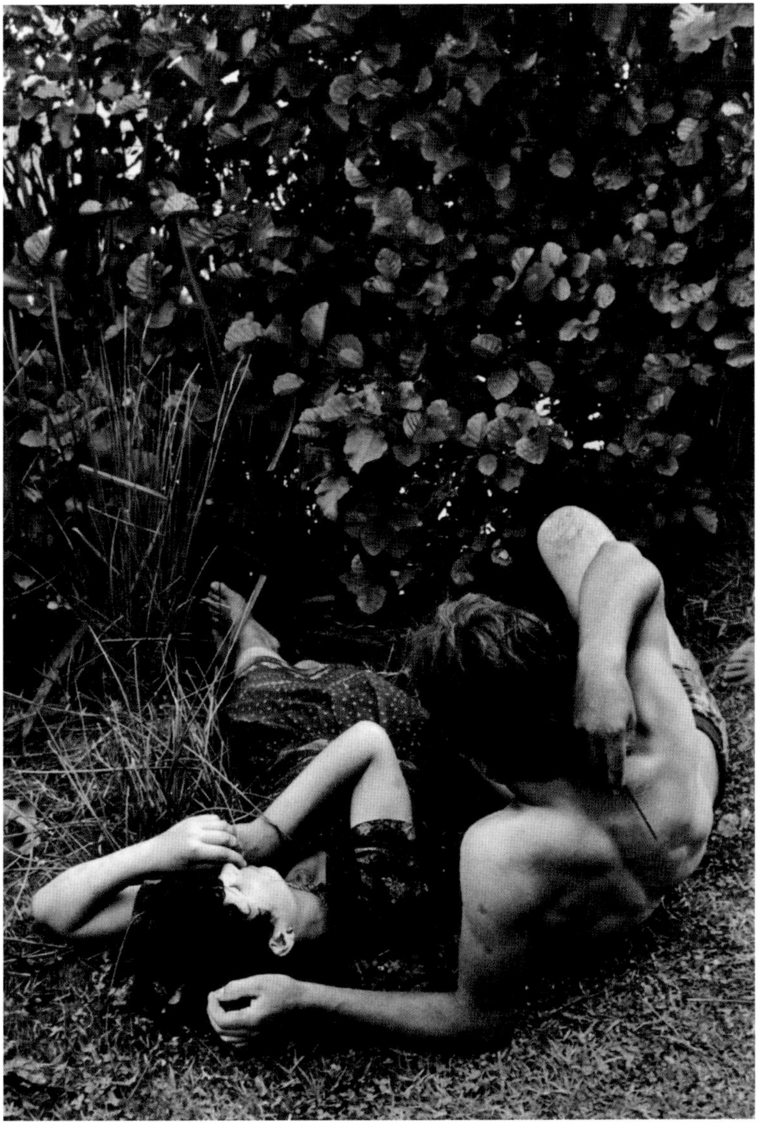

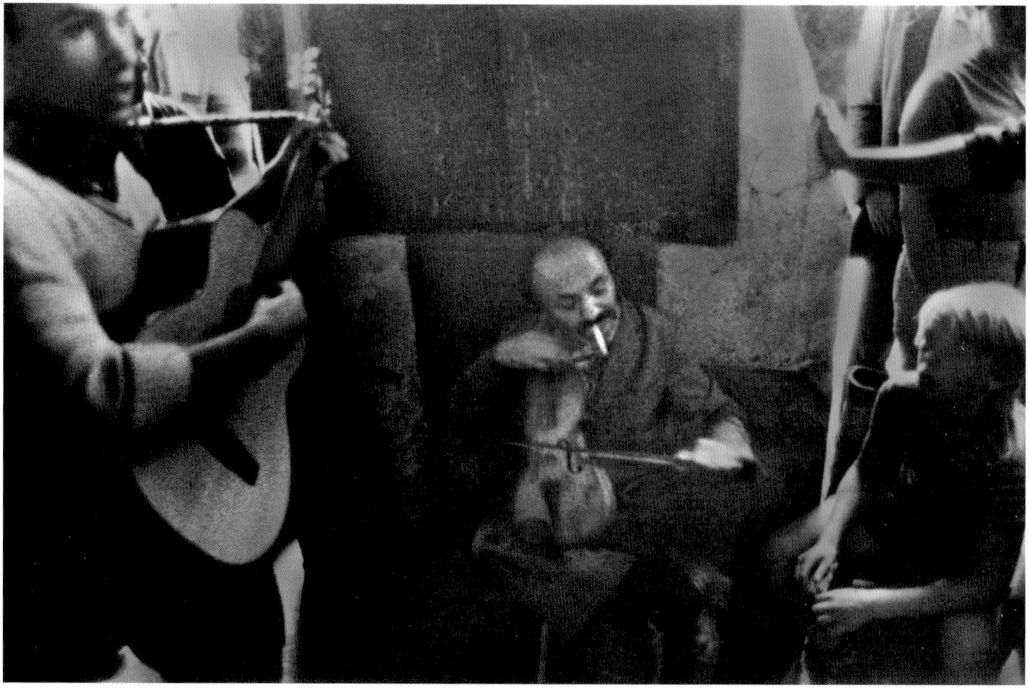

39 **Cracow / Krakov, Poland / Polsko** 1986

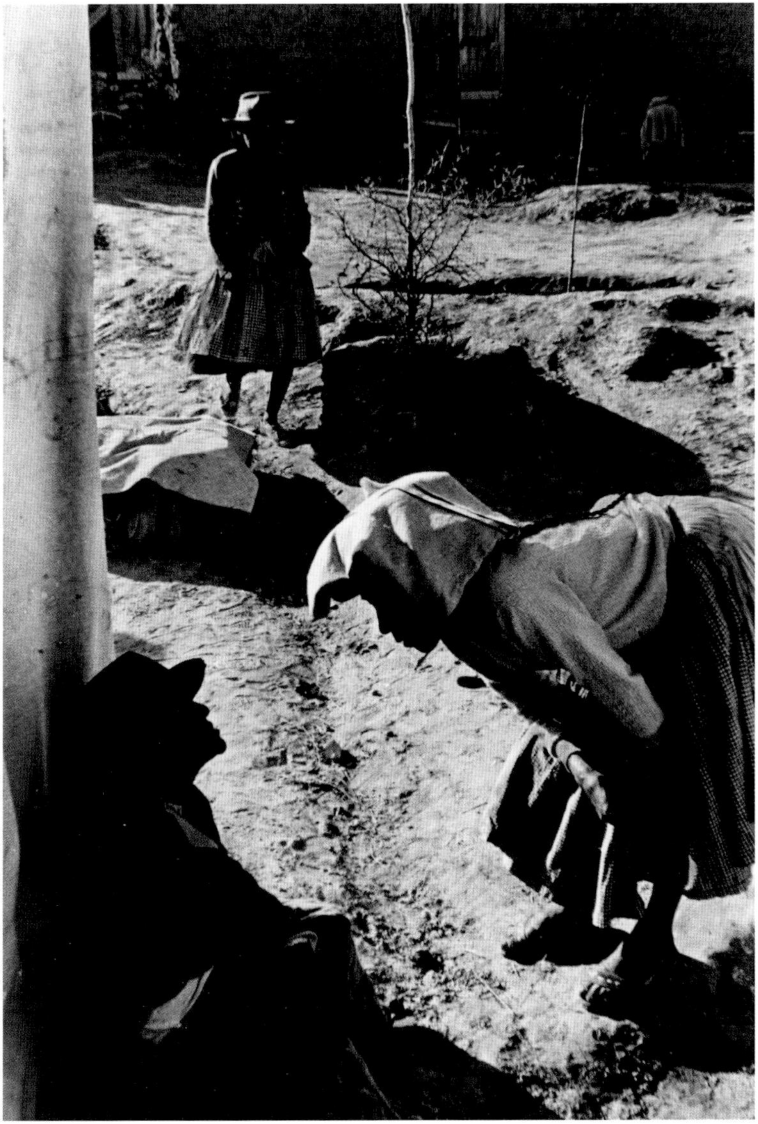

40 **Humahuaca, Argentina** 1983

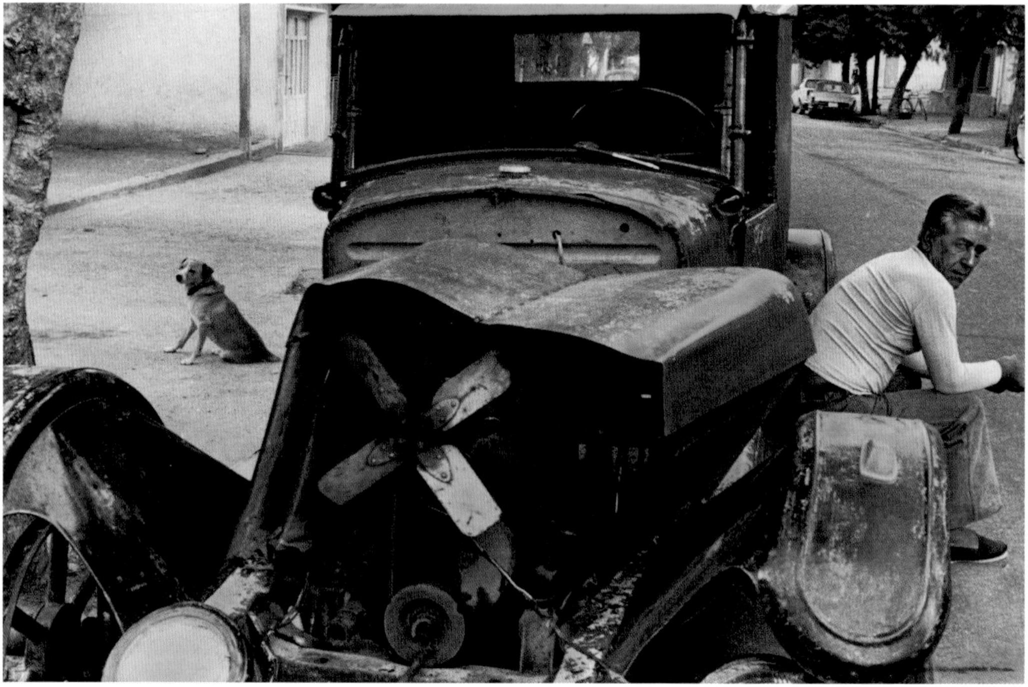

41 **Colonia del Sacramento, Uruguay** 1983

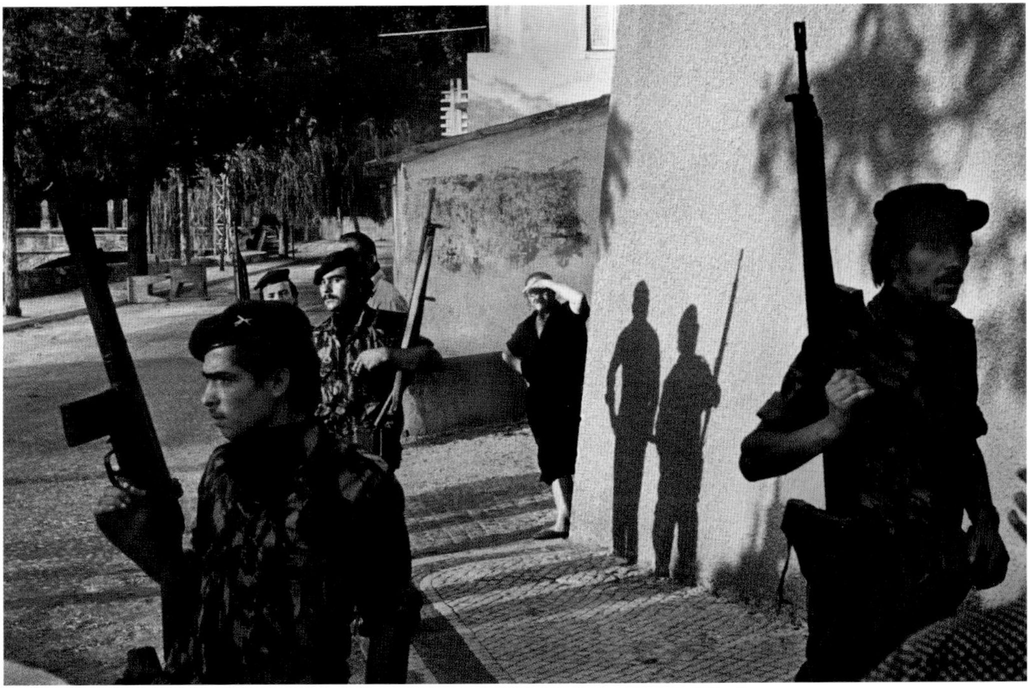

42 **Leiria, Portugal / Portugalsko** 1975

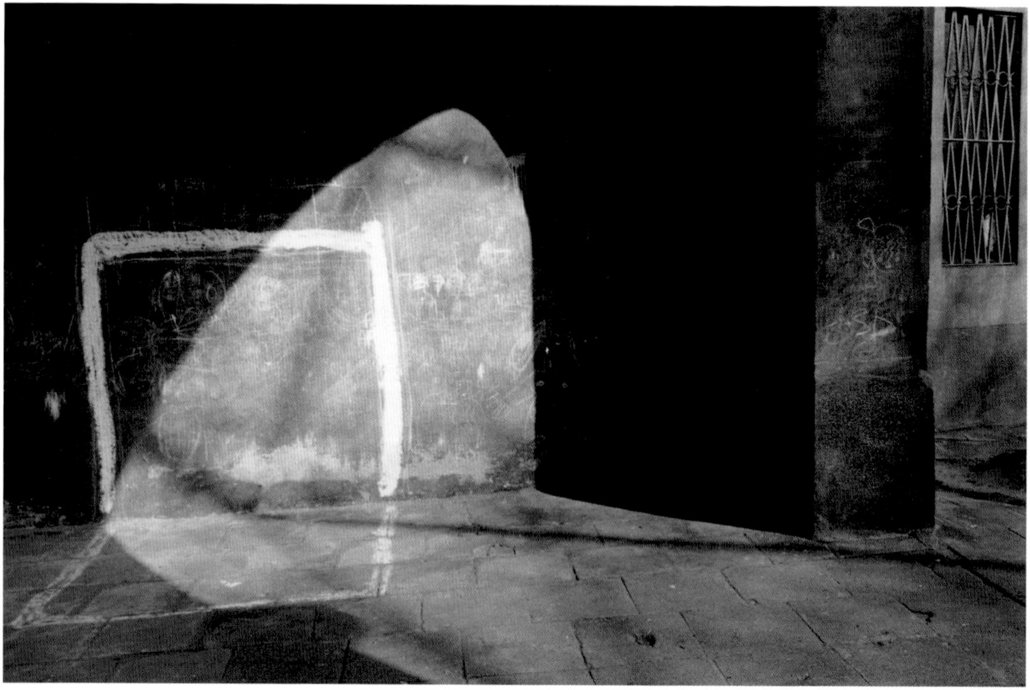

43 **Łódź, Poland / Polsko** 1988

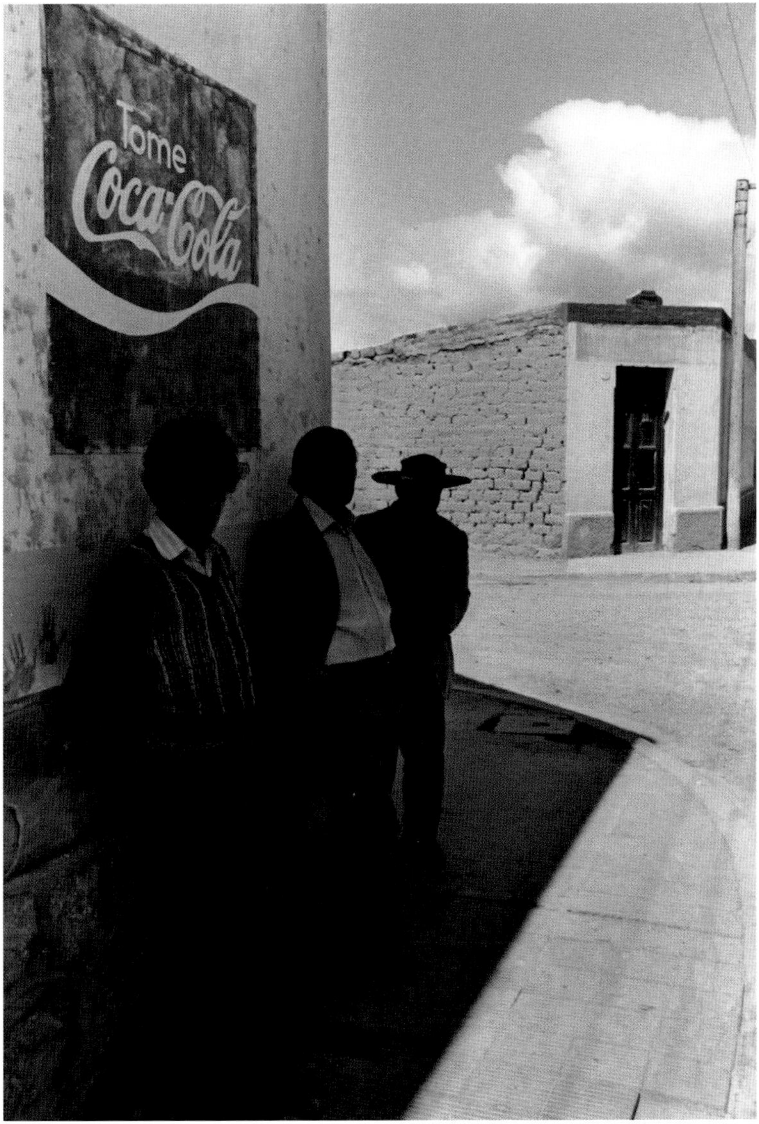

44 **Humahuaca, Argentina** 1983

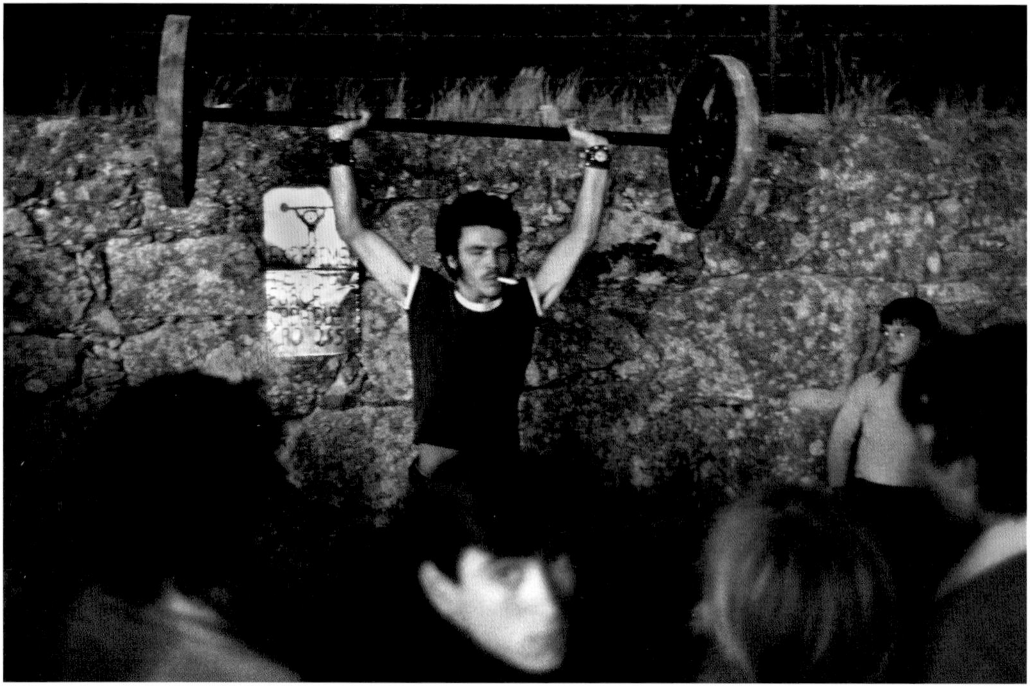

45 **Viana do Castelo, Portugal / Portugalsko** 1977

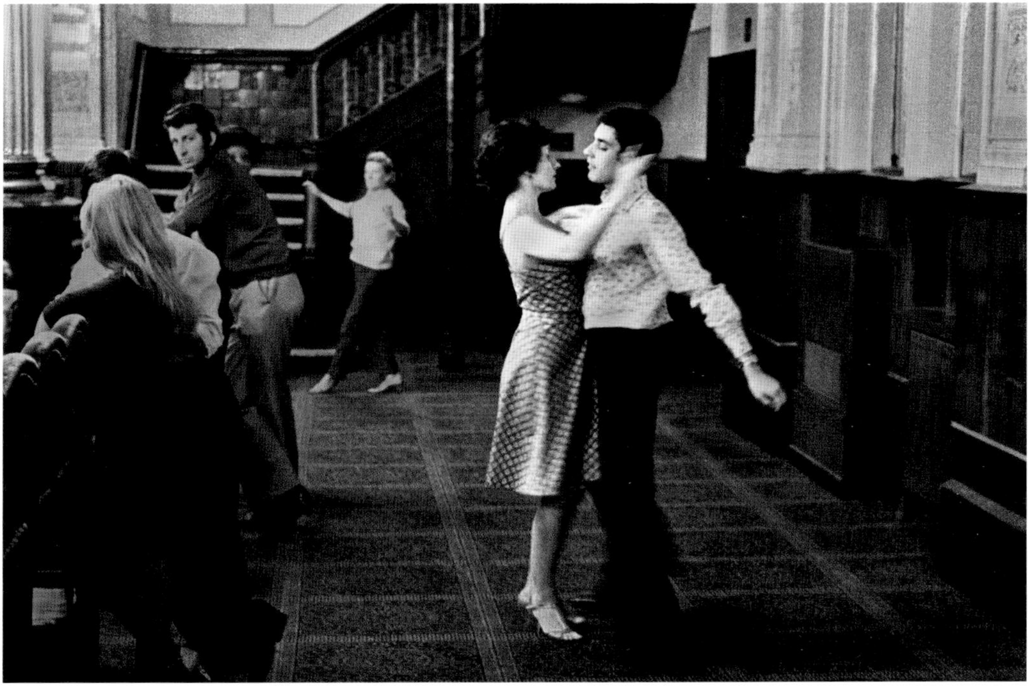

46 **Blackpool, Great Britain / Velká Británie** 1978

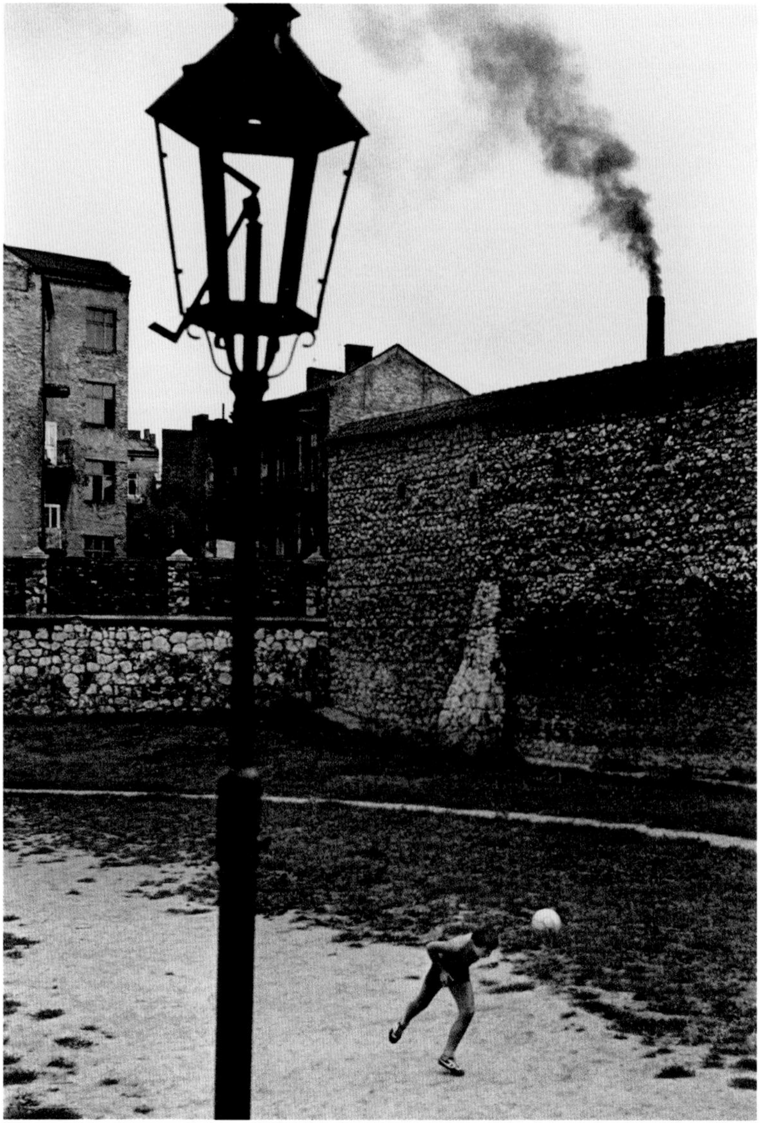

47 **Cracow / Krakov, Poland / Polsko** 1986

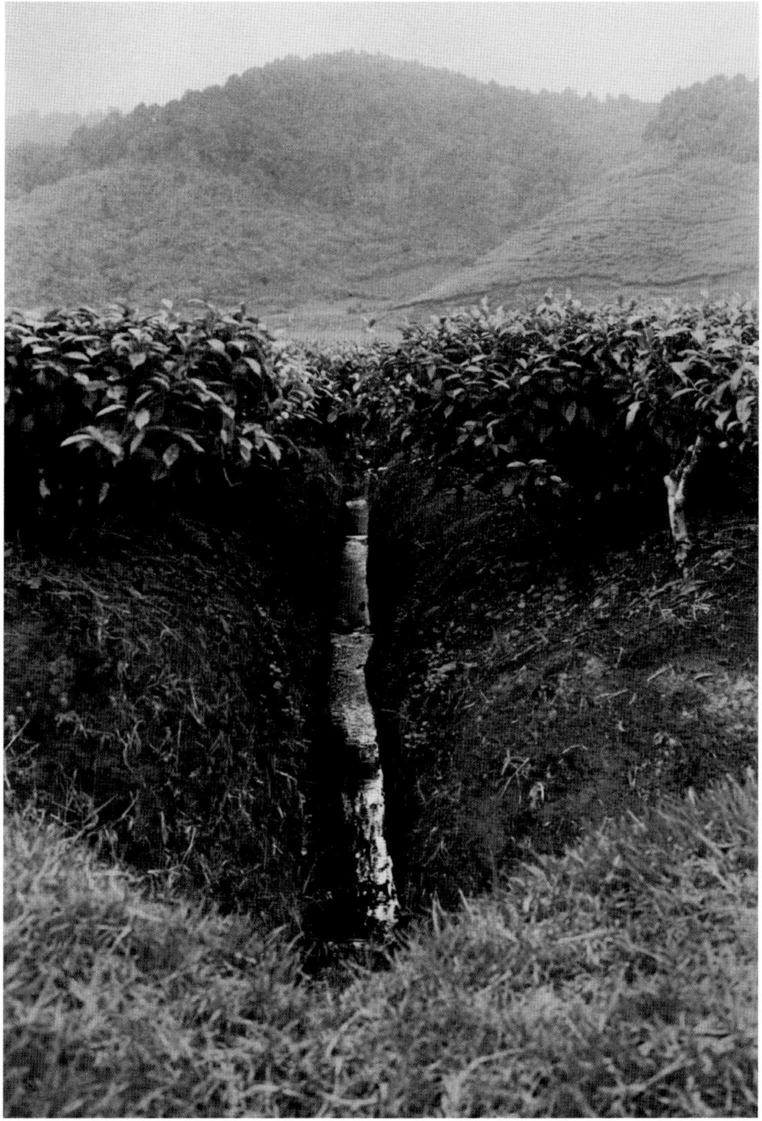

48 **Java, Indonesia / Indonésie** 1982

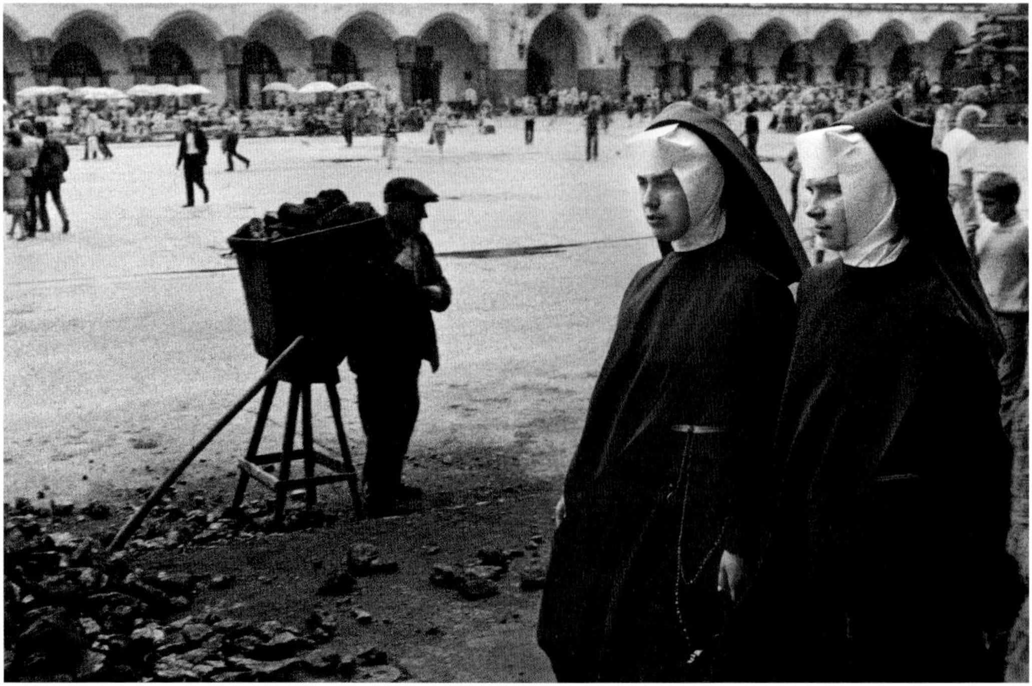

49 **Cracow / Krakov, Poland / Polsko** 1982

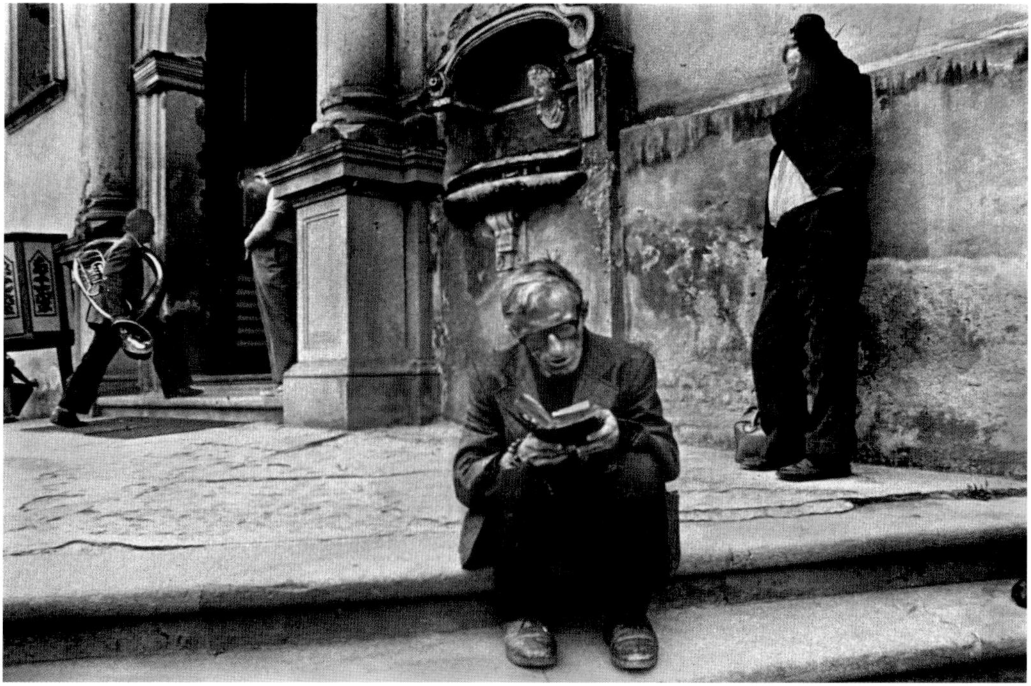

50 **Kalwaria Zebrzydowska, Poland / Polsko** 1984

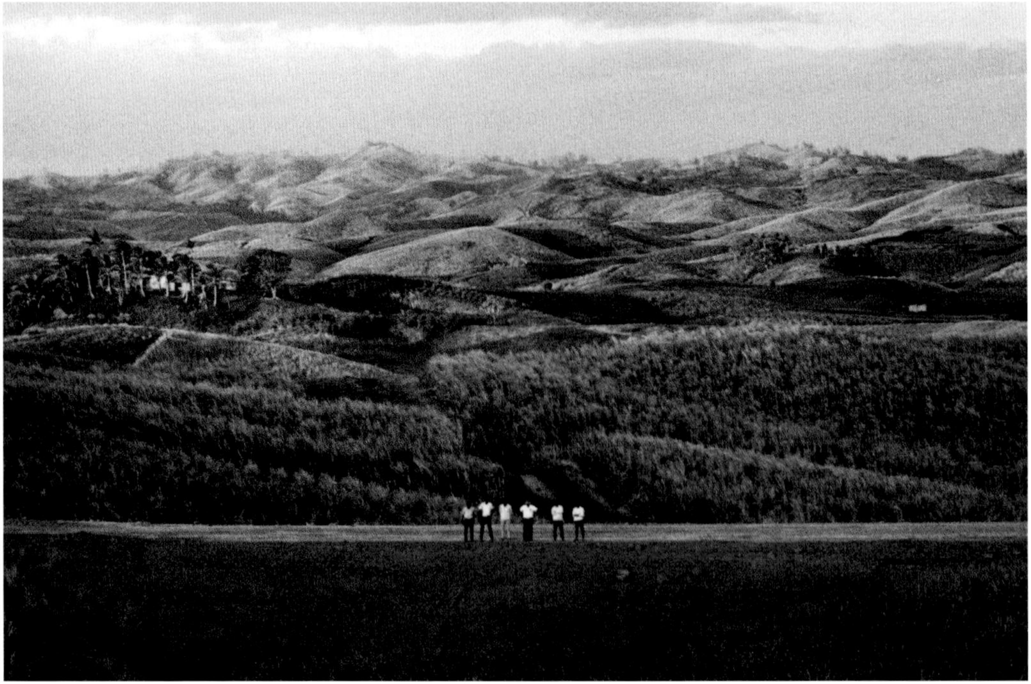

51 **Fiji / Ostrovy Fidži** 1973

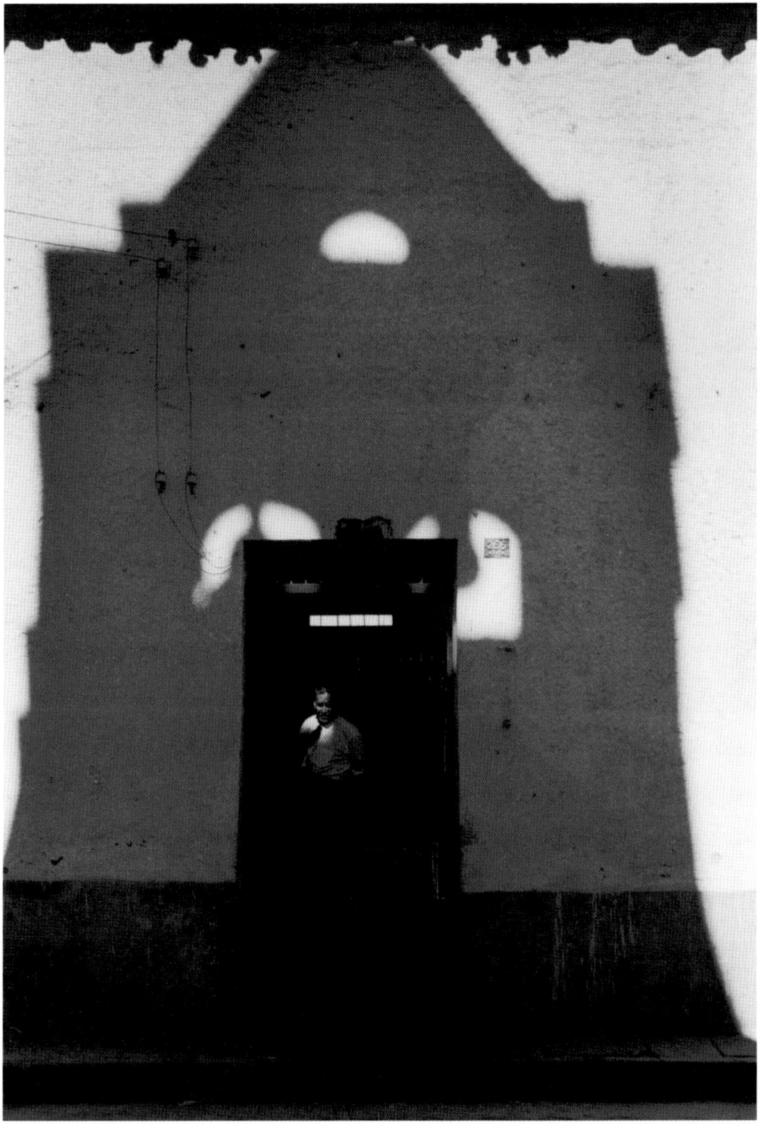

52 **Potosí, Bolivia / Bolívie** 1983

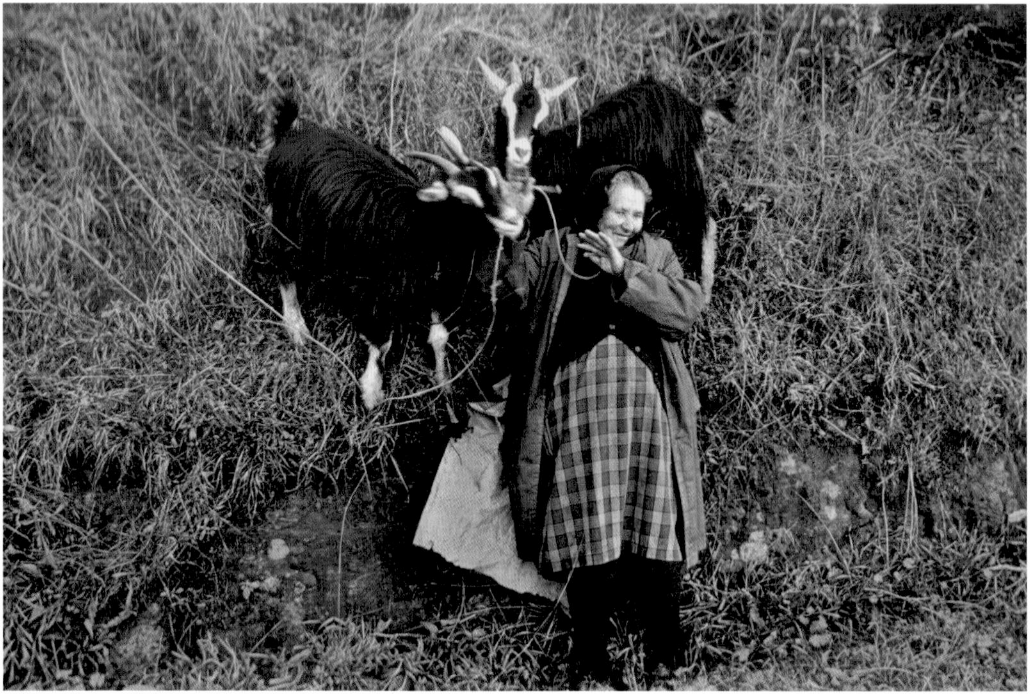

53 **Portugal / Portugalsko**

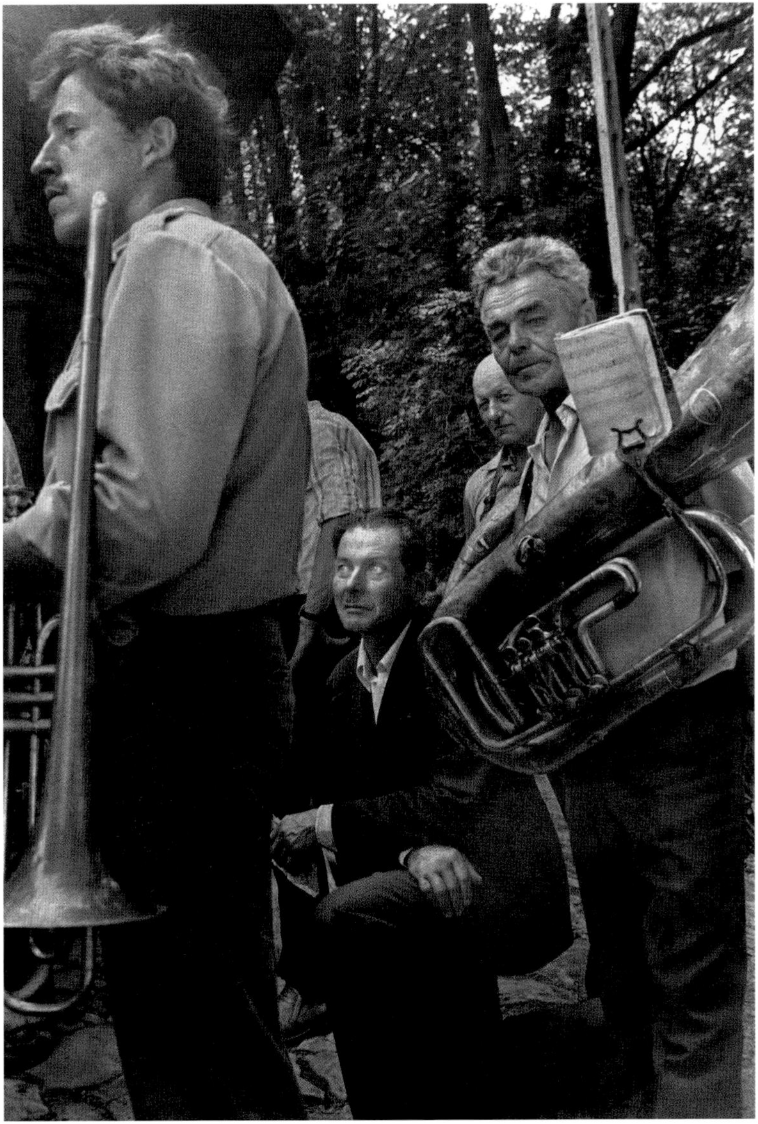

54 **Kalwaria Zebrzydowska, Poland / Polsko** 1986

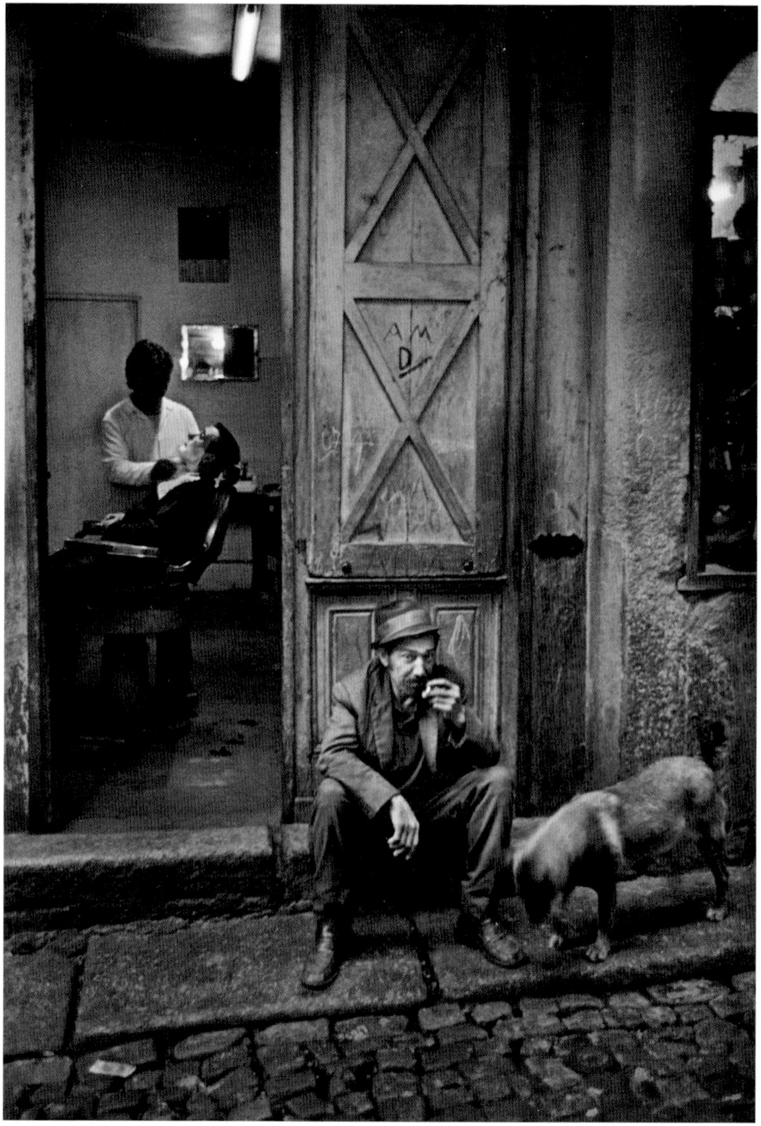

55 **Porto, Portugal / Portugalsko** 1978

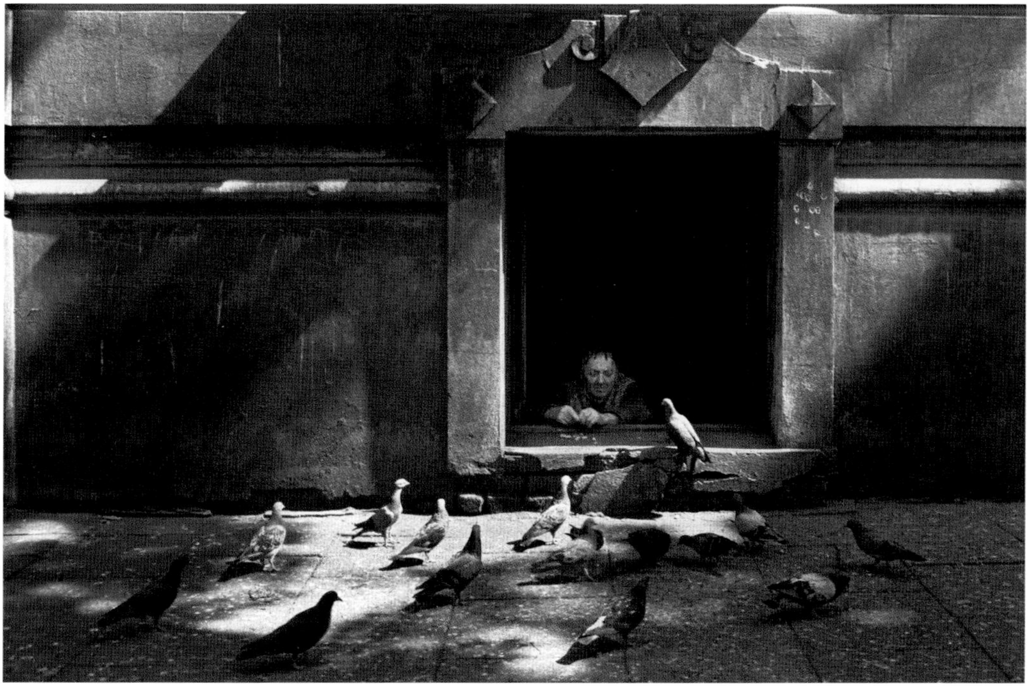

56 **Cracow / Krakov, Poland / Polsko** 1982

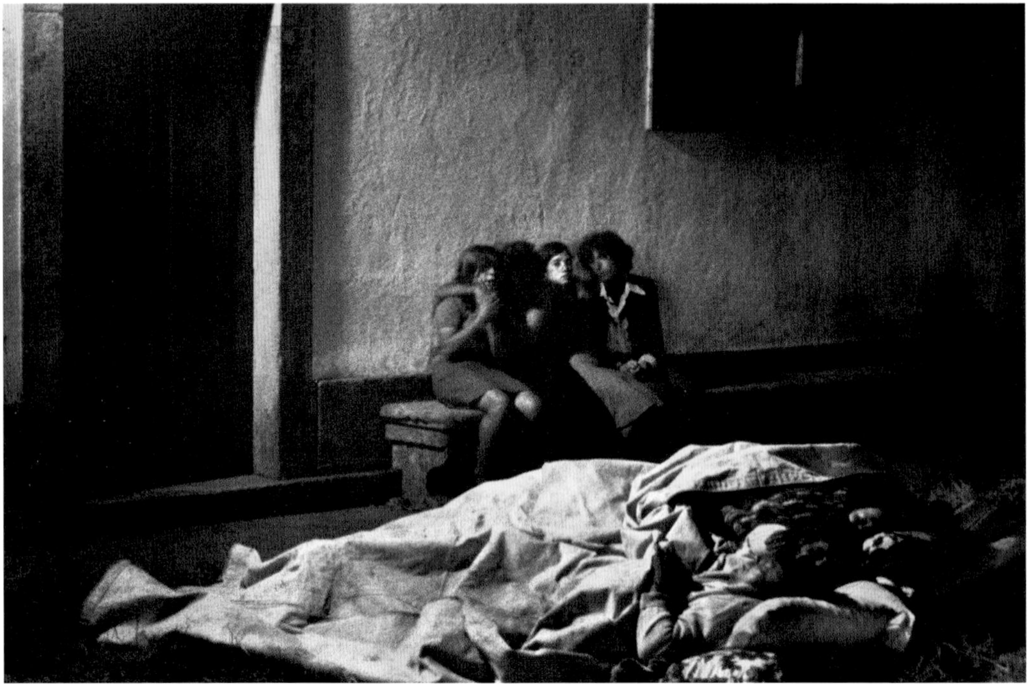

57 **Viana do Castelo, Portugal / Portugalsko** 1975

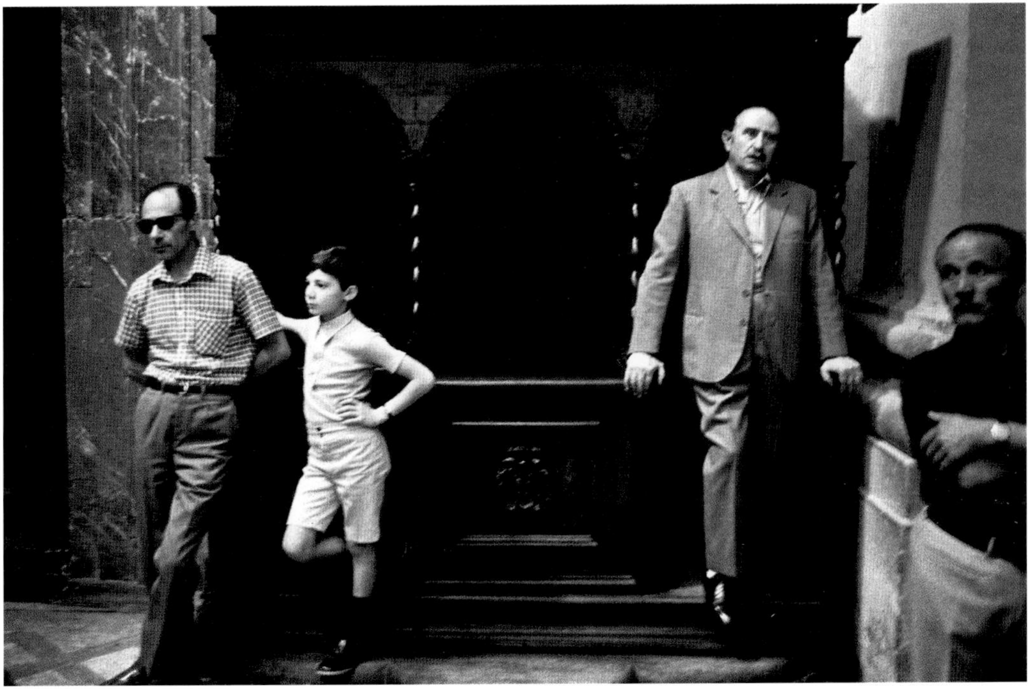

58 **Spoleto, Italy / Itálie** 1974

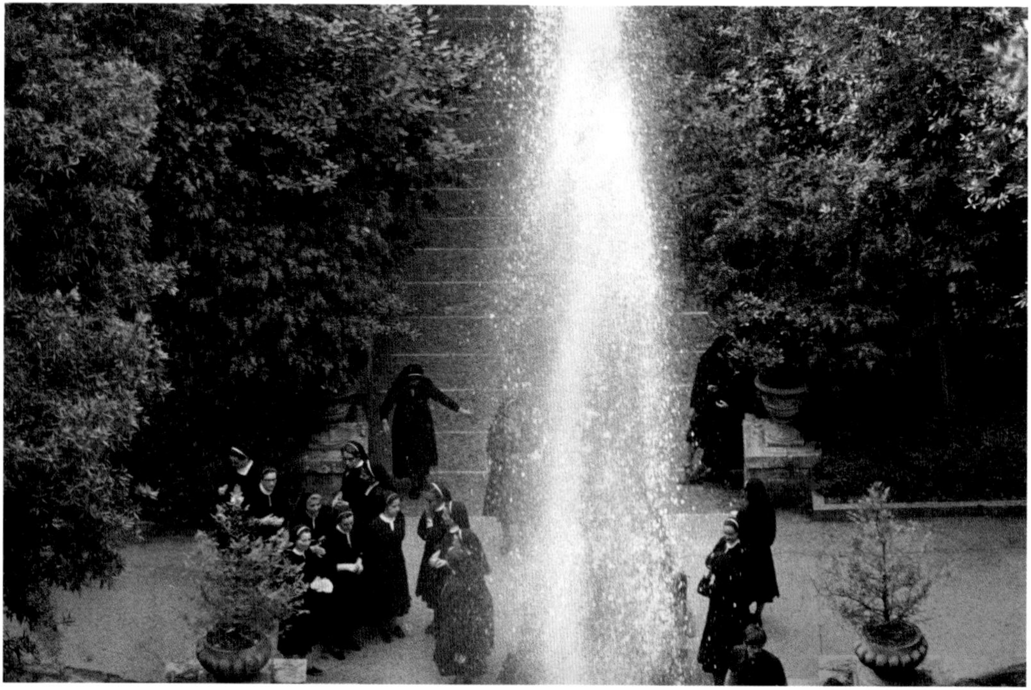

59 **Castel Gandolfo, Italy / Itálie** 1972

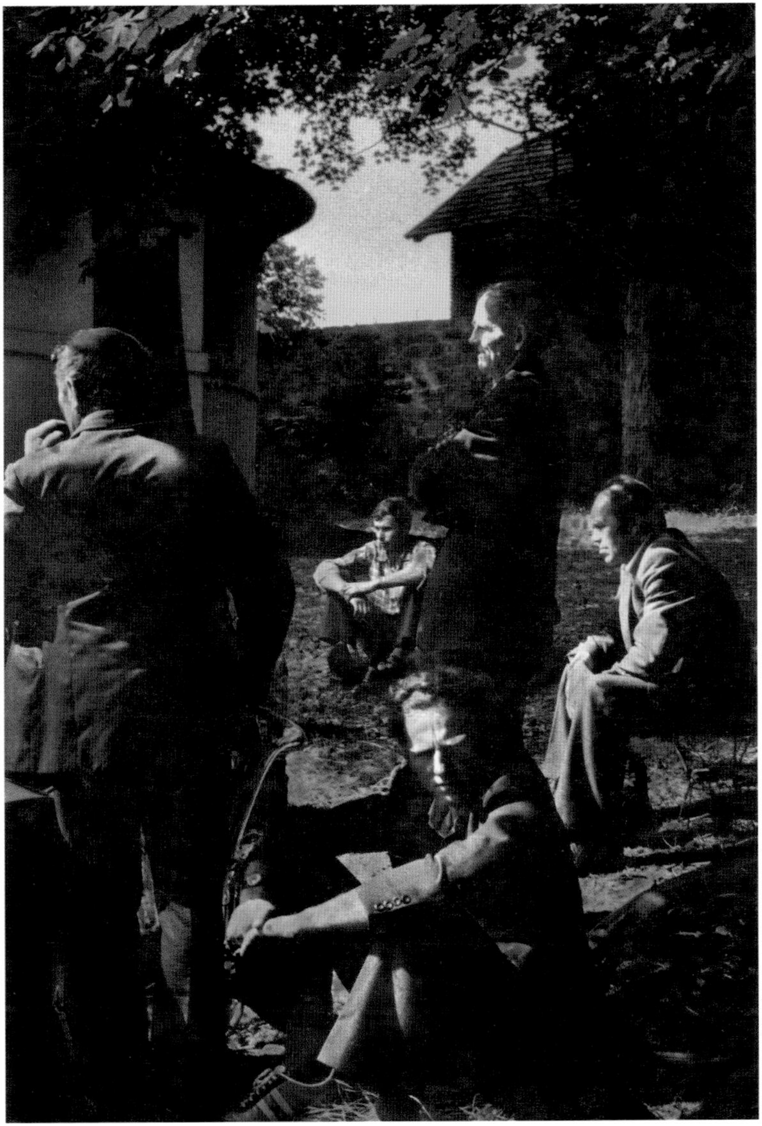

60 **Kalwaria Zebrzydowska, Poland / Polsko** 1986

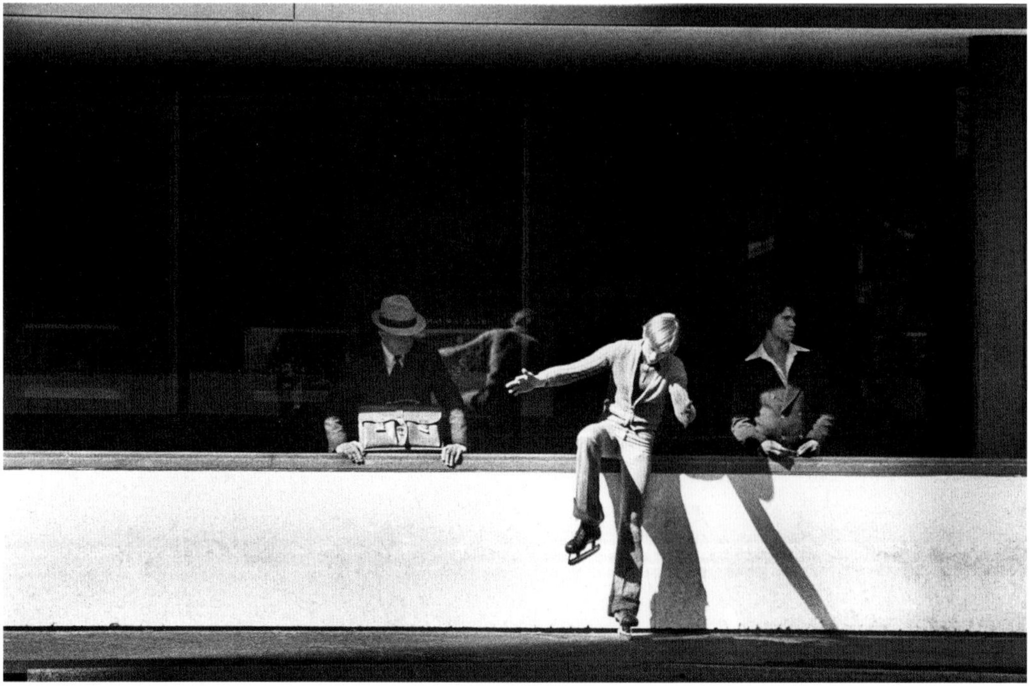

61 **Berlin / Berlín, Germany / Německo** 1973

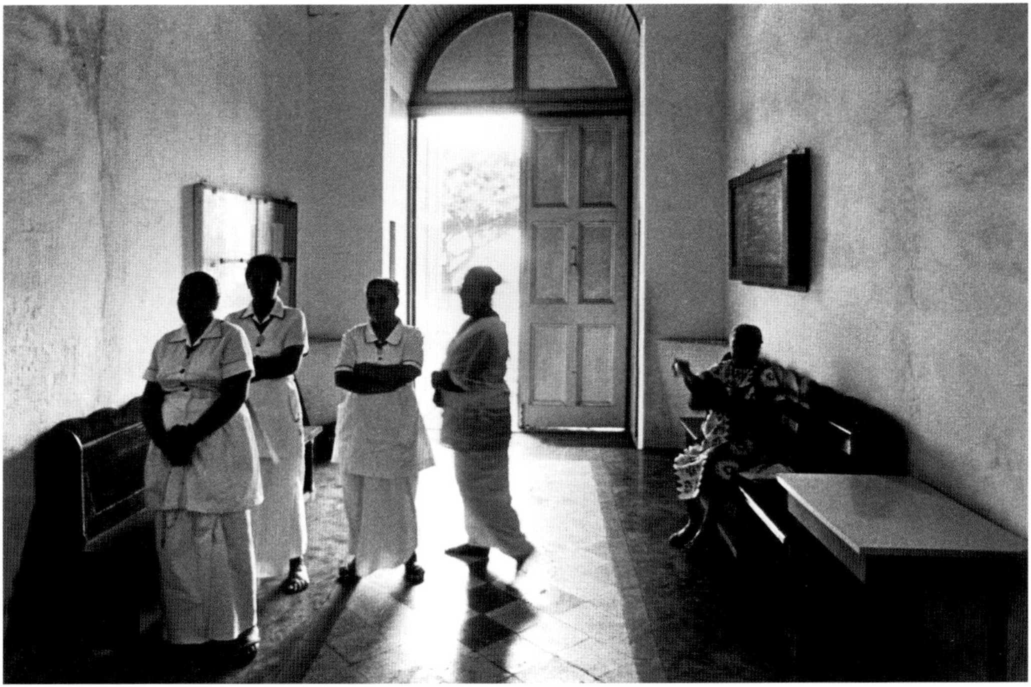

62 **American Samoa / Americká Samoa** 1973

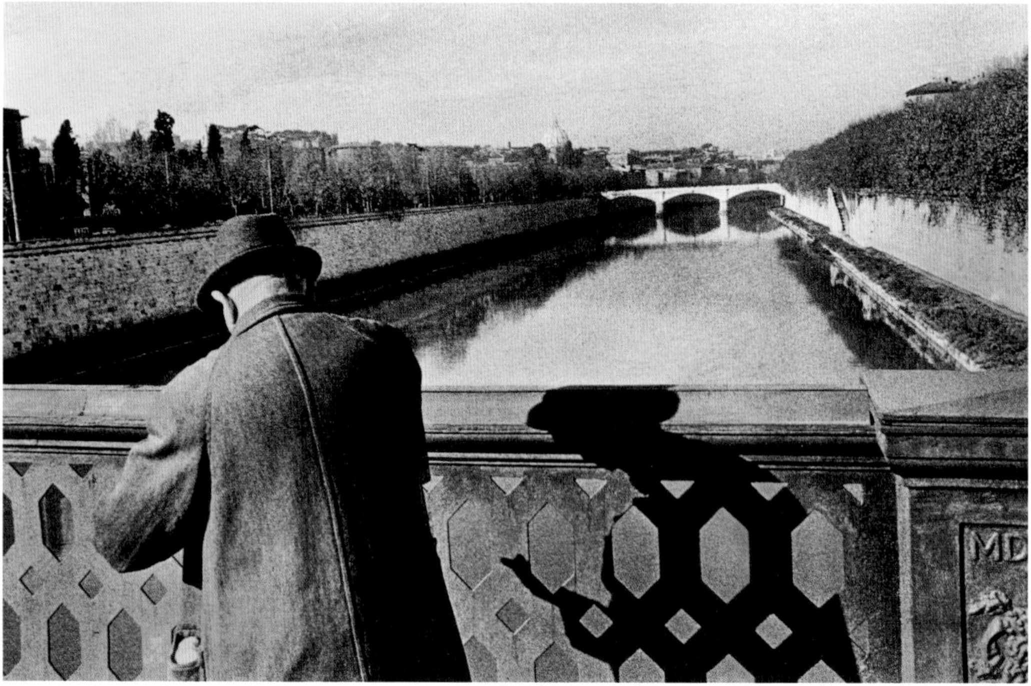

63 **Rome / Řím, Italy / Itálie** 1974

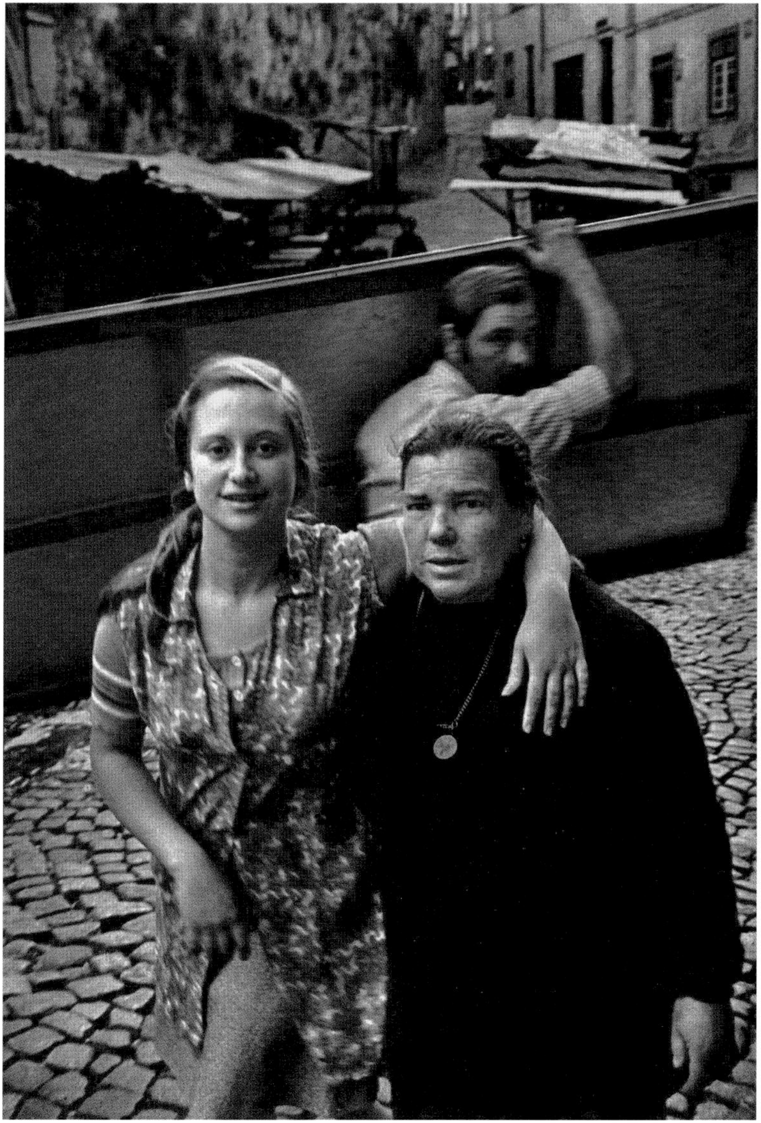

64 **Porto, Portugal / Portugalsko** 1977

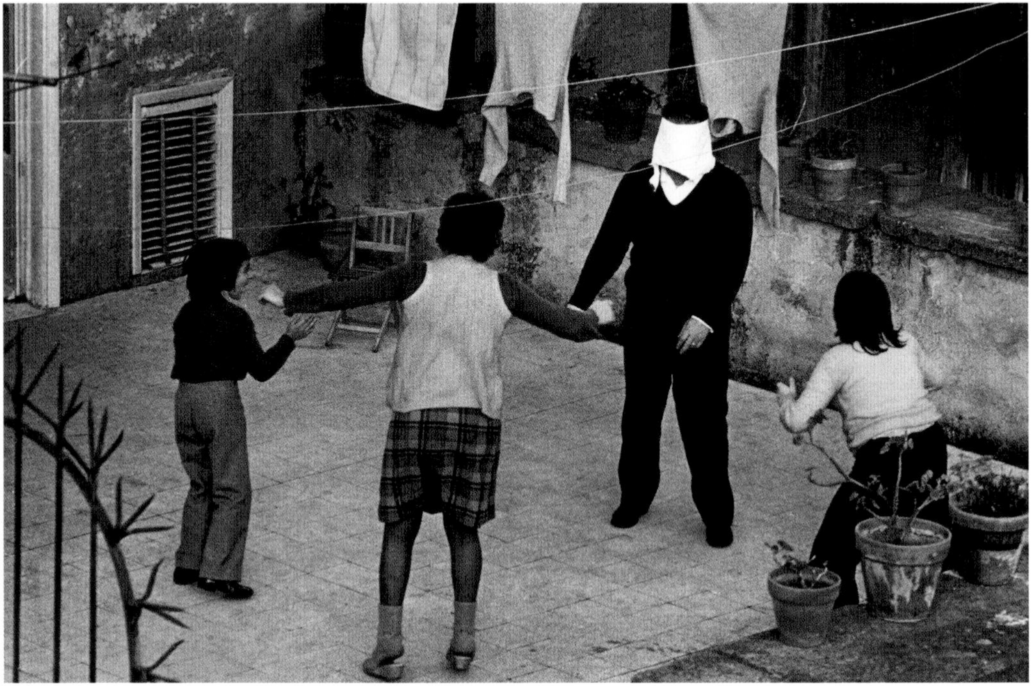

65 **Rome / Řím, Italy / Itálie** 1972

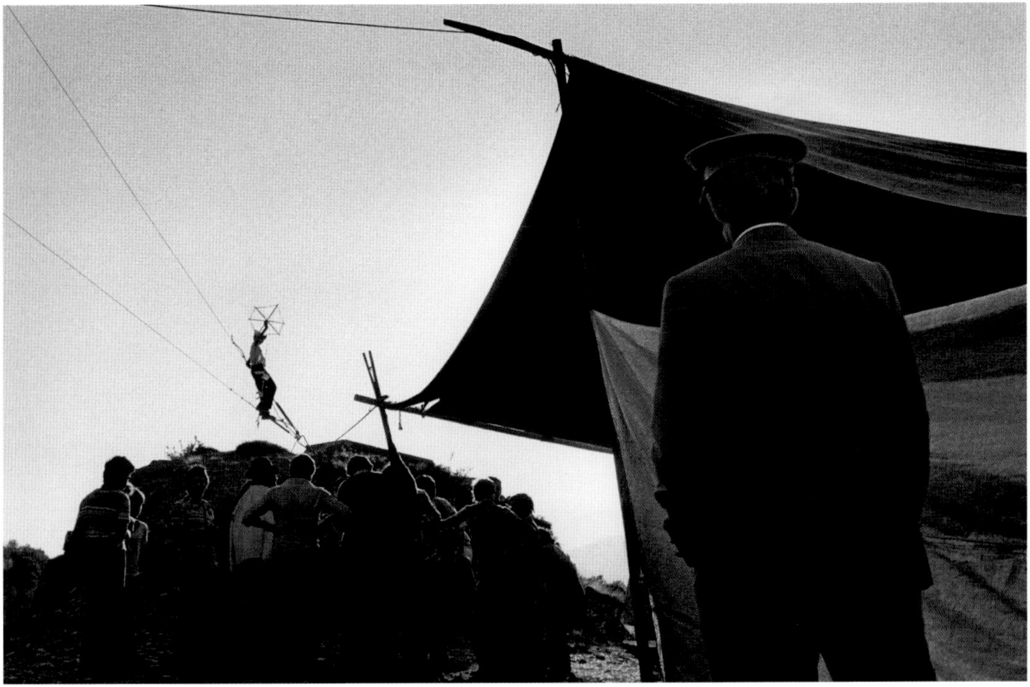

66 **Mondim de Basto, Portugal / Portugalsko** 1977

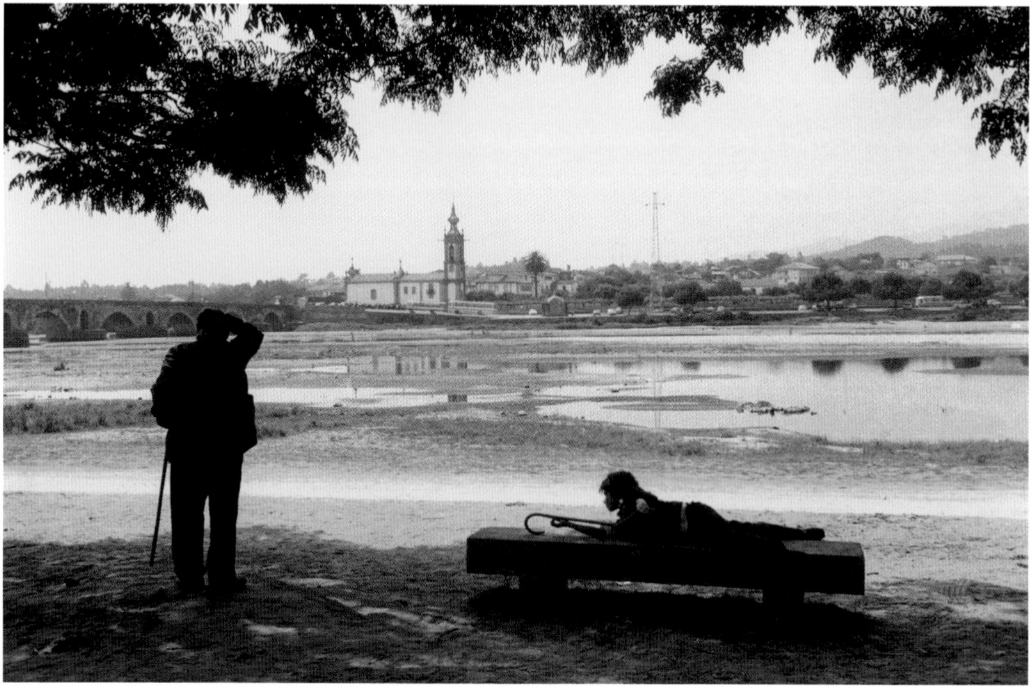

67 **Ponte de Lima, Portugal / Portugalsko** 1976

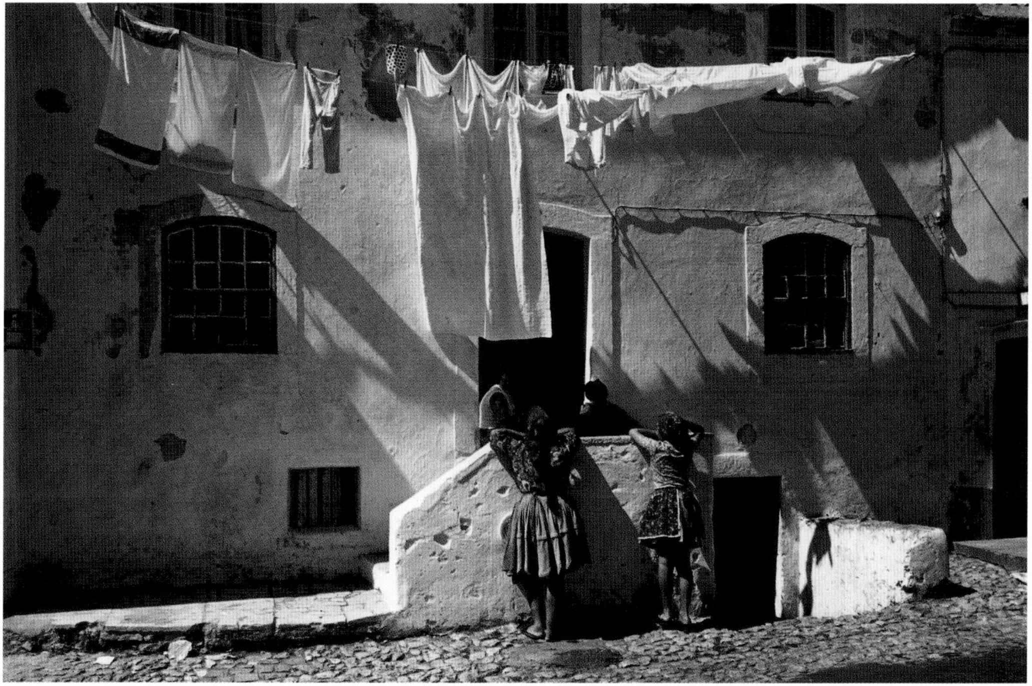

68 **Nazaré, Portugal / Portugalsko** 1978

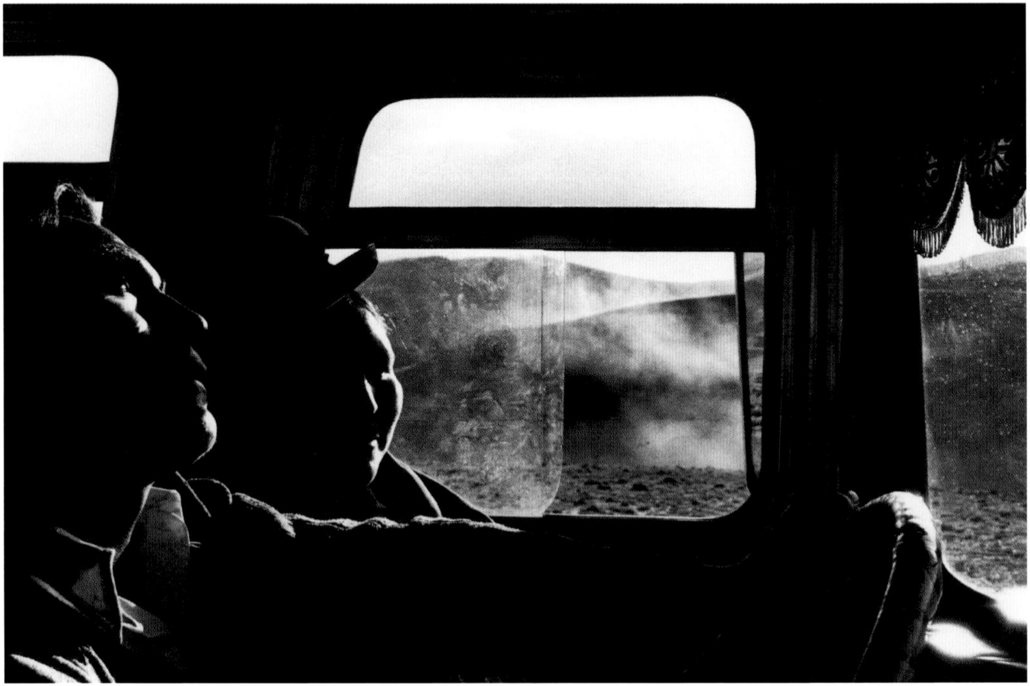

69 **Near La Paz / Poblíž La Pazu, Bolivia / Bolívie** 1983

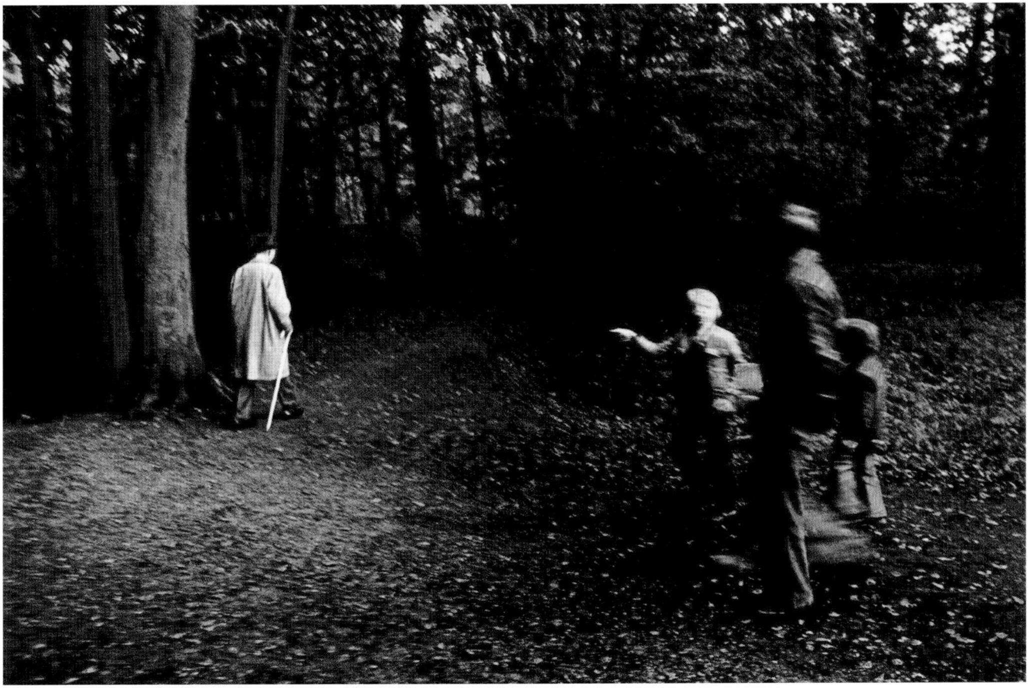

70 **Clingendael, The Hague, the Netherlands / Den Haag, Nizozemí** 1974

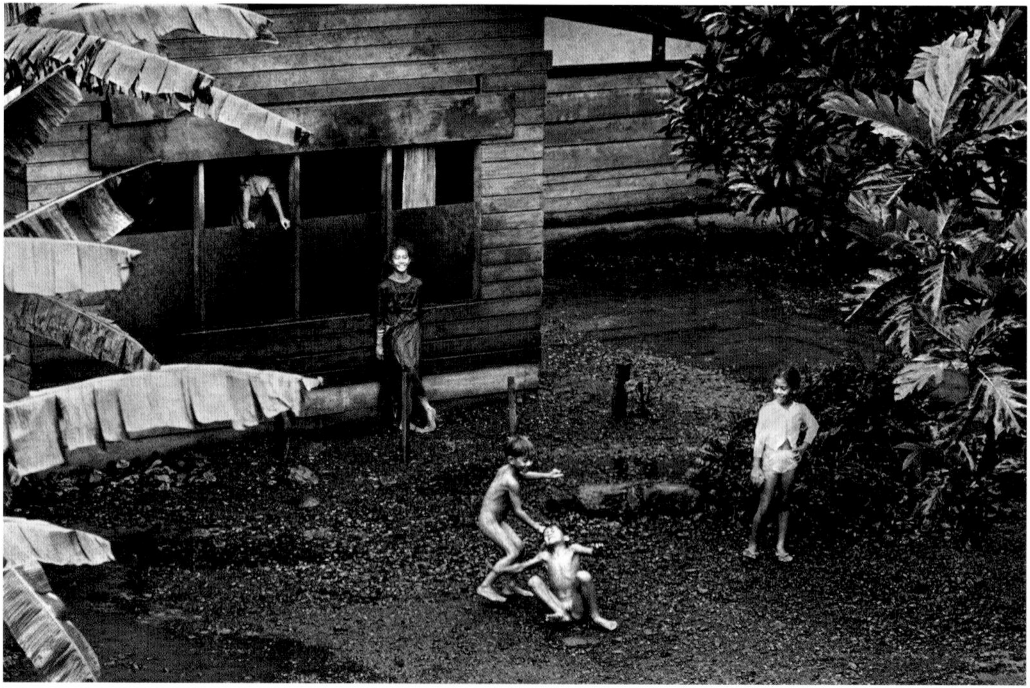

71 **Western Samoa / Západní Samoa** 1973

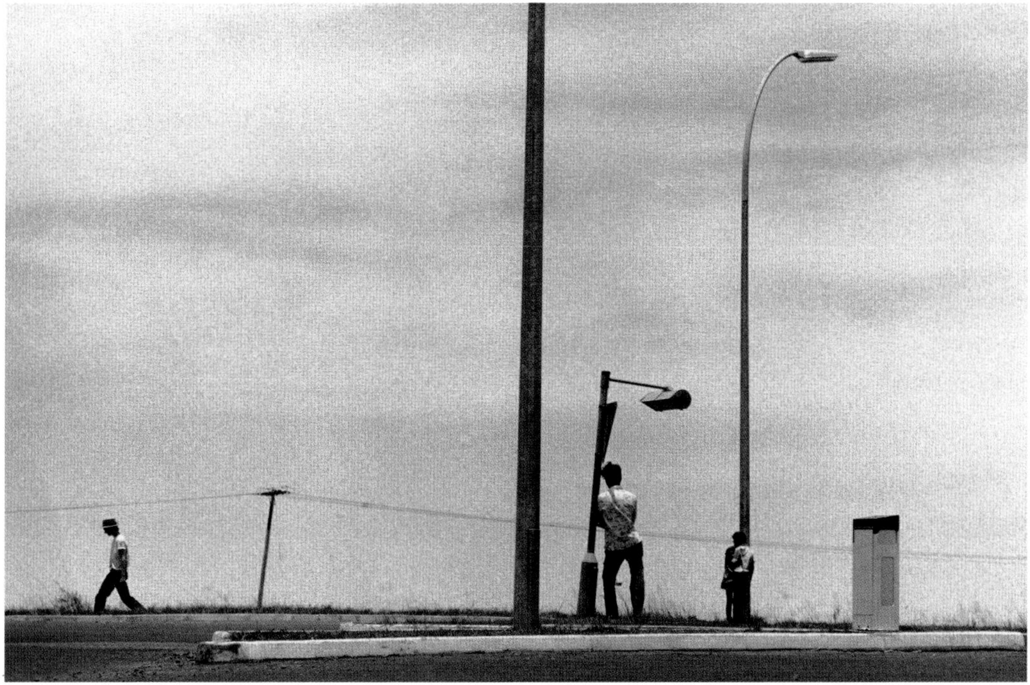

72 **Suva, Fiji / Ostrovy Fidži** 1973

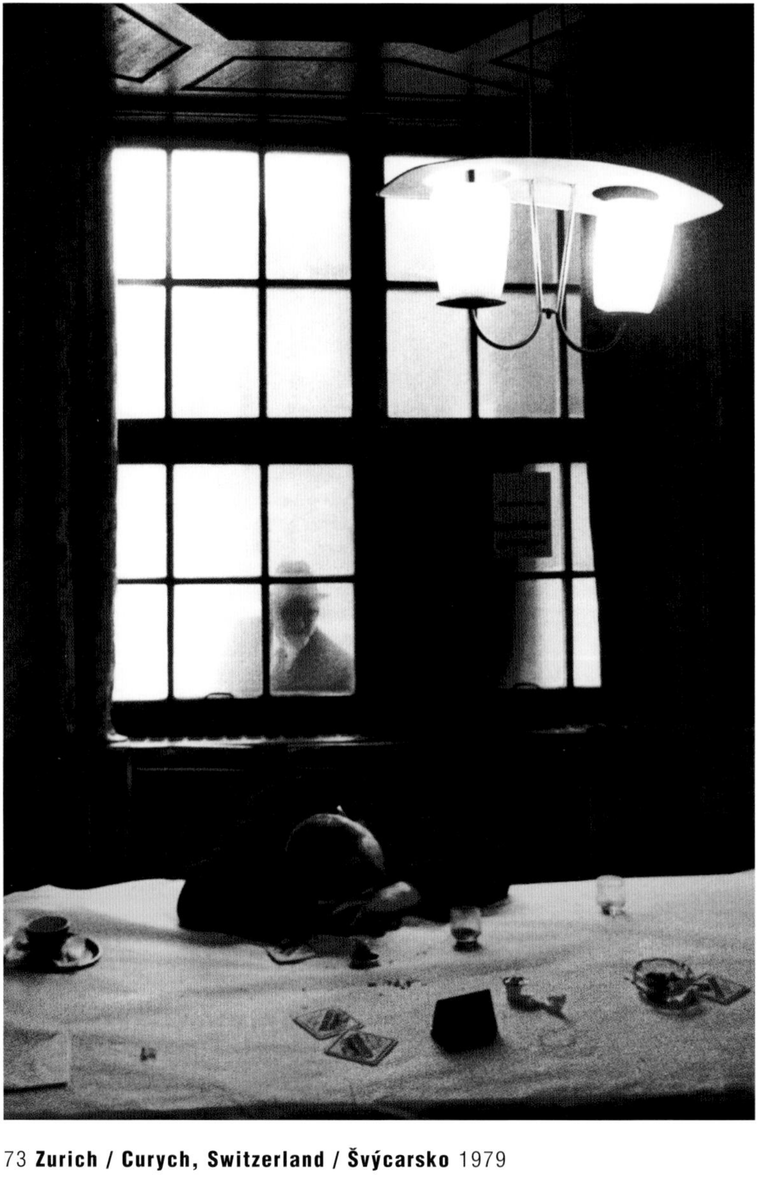

73 **Zurich / Curych, Switzerland / Švýcarsko** 1979

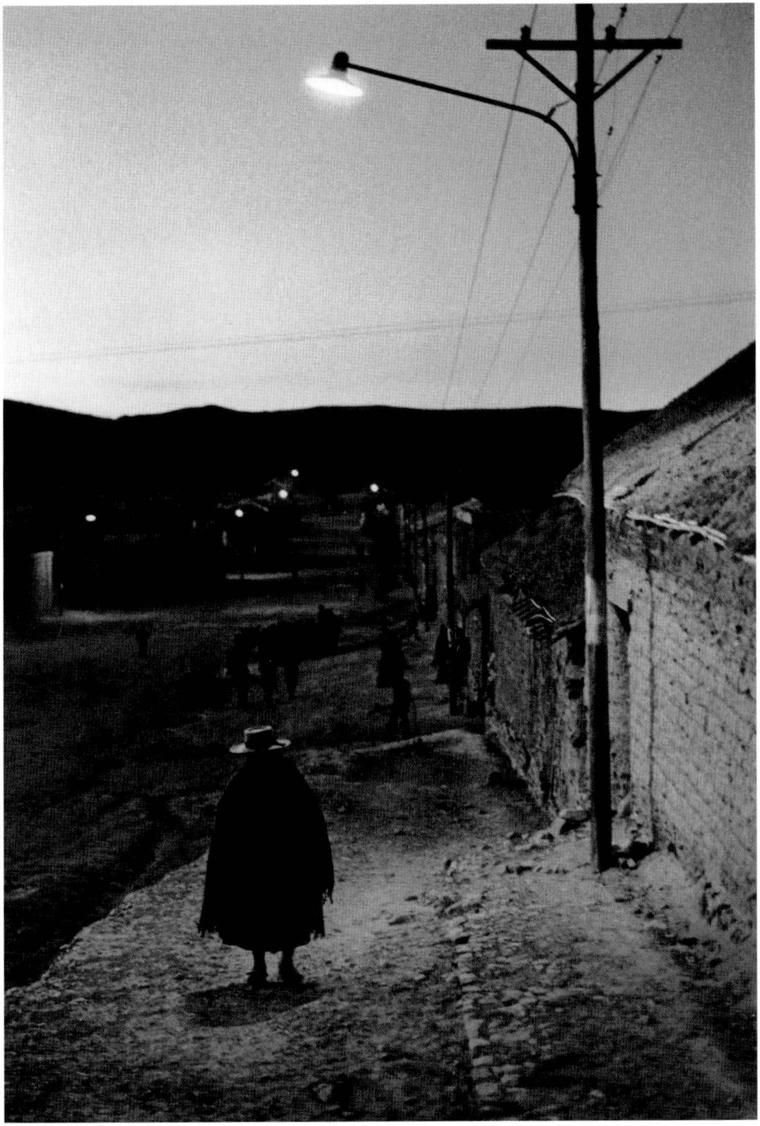

74 **Humahuaca, Argentina** 1983

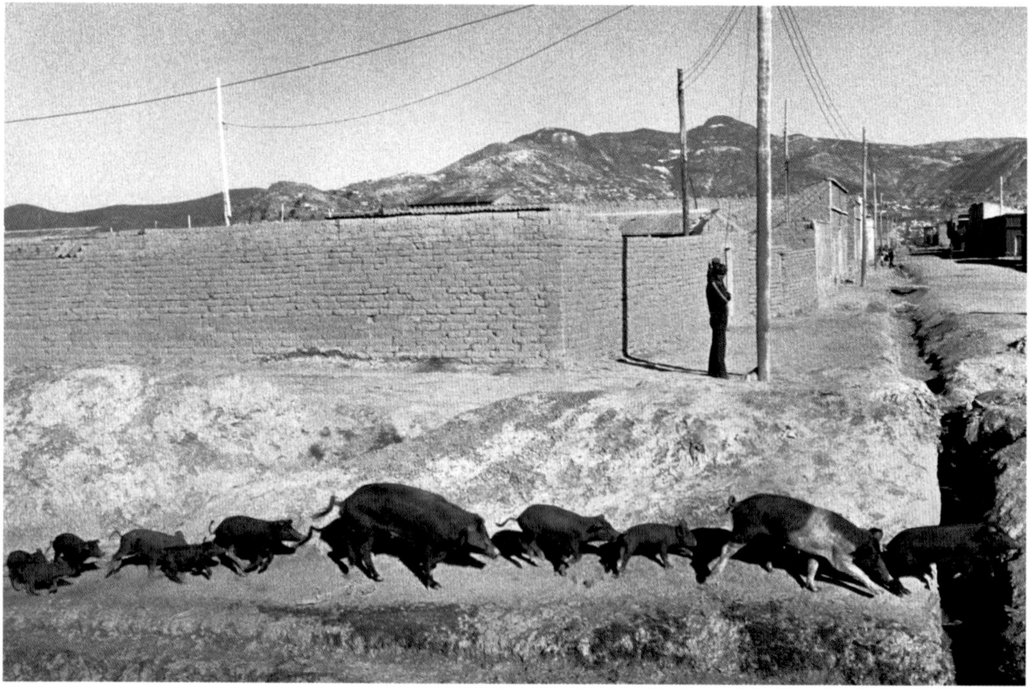

75 **Oruro, Bolivia / Bolívie** 1983

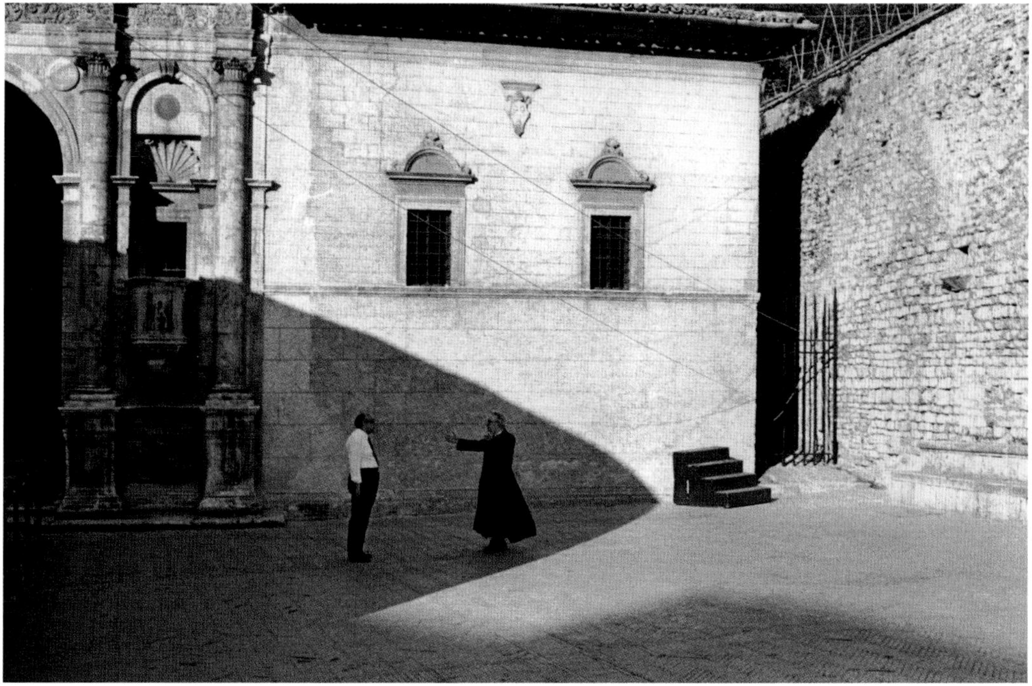

76 **Spoleto, Italy / Itálie** 1974

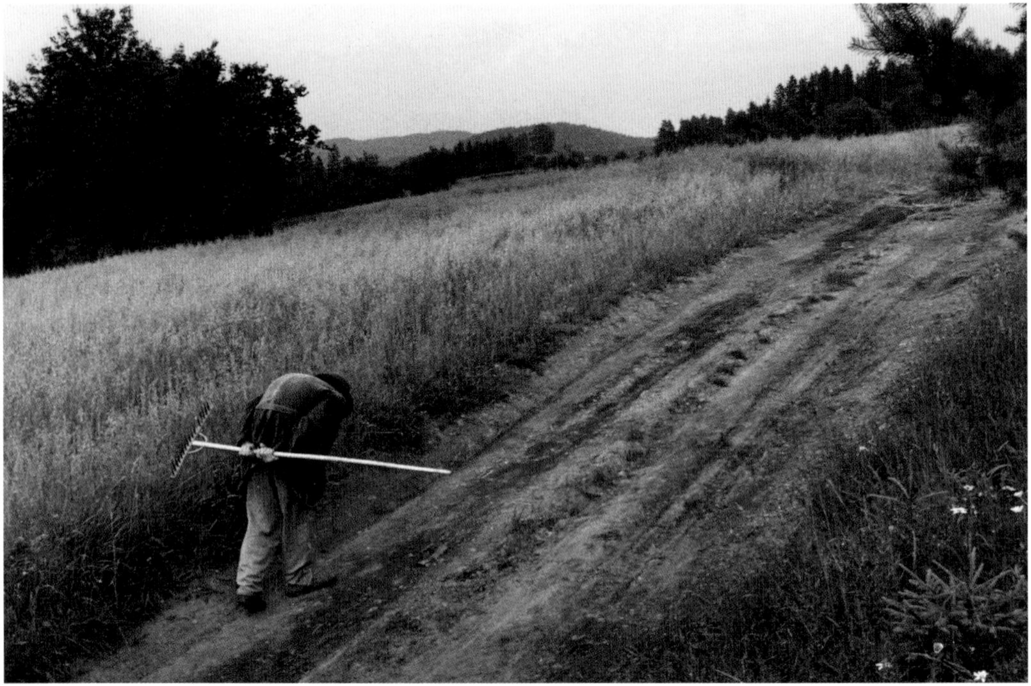

77 **Near Vizovice / Poblíž Vizovic, Moravia / Morava** 1988

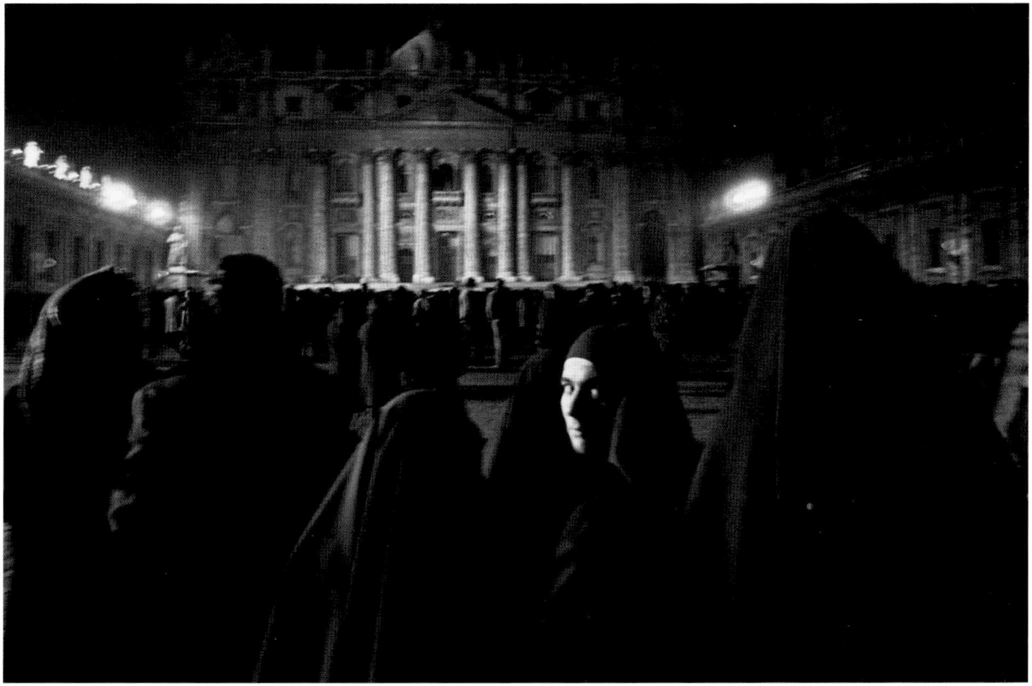

78 **Vatican City / Vatikán** 1974

Biographical Chronology

1947 Born on 12 June, in Brno, to Emil and Marie Dukát. His mother was a teacher, his father a development engineer (specialized in Zetor tractors) and an amateur photographer who developed and printed the family photographs. Vojta has a sister and a brother.

1953–62 Went to school in Hroznova ulice, Brno, and finished elementary school in Křídlovická ulice, Brno.

1962–65 Attended the Brno college of electronic engineering. The underage constructor of Audion receivers with positive feedback did not finish his studies, but did learn to use his father's Voigtländer bellows camera and became a traveler and an observer of the world. Got a Lubitel camera.

1966 Worked as a stagehand at the Mahen Theater, Brno, then at the Janáček Opera House, Brno. At his own request, was admitted to a psychiatric hospital, was unable to perform compulsory military service. He was later hired part time to photograph experimental group therapy at the clinic.

1967–68 Held various jobs and moved from the Moravian capital to the Bohemian capital. He repaired gas pumps, worked as a model at the Academy of Fine Arts, Prague, and worked again as a stagehand, this time at the E. F. Burian Theater, Prague.

1968 Beginning in January, he was an assistant lighting technician for Czechoslovak Television news, in order to gain practical experience when applying for training as a camera operator at the Film and Television School of the Academy of Performing Arts (FAMU), Prague. "Sometimes I was allowed," he says today, "to load film into an Eclair 16 mm camera." In the spring, he got his first 35 mm camera. In the summer, he took up an invitation to visit friends in the Netherlands. After the occupation of Czechoslovakia by five Warsaw Pact armies, he remained in exile in the Netherlands.

1968–70 Studied photography at the Gerrit Rietveld Academie, Amsterdam. His teacher, Jaap d'Oliveira, fearing that Dukát would not pass the first year, accepted him straight into the second year at the photography department.

1969 Was granted refugee status in the Netherlands and given papers for stateless people to travel freely. Visited West Berlin several times.

1970–71 Left the Rietveld Academie for the Netherlands Film Academy in Amsterdam, where he began training as a cameraman, but left near the end of the first year.

1972–73 Was often in Rome, and also visited friends in Zurich, Paris, and London. Started a trip around the world but, "for financial reasons, unfortunately, had to do it in less than 80 days."

1974 In New York City, met the 80-year-old photographer André Kertész, who put him in touch with Magnum Photos in New York City. Here, first made contact with Elliott Erwitt and René Burri. Was a Nominee of Magnum Photos in Paris, where he was in touch with Bruno Barbey.

1975 Worked on a project documenting the city of Amsterdam. First visited Portugal, where Magnum had sent him to photograph the first elections after the Carnation Revolution.

Among other things, also photographed carnivals in the Federal Republic of Germany and Switzerland and competitions of ballroom dancers in the Netherlands, Belgium, and Great Britain.

1976 Acquired Dutch citizenship and was given a grant from the Ministry of Culture of the Netherlands to document the problem of alienation. Became a Magnum Nominee for a second time. In Hungary, met with his family for the first time in eight years. Visited Yugoslavia and returned to Portugal.

1977 As a documentary photographer, recorded the experimental therapy of drug addicts in the Netherlands. In New York, got an OM camera from Olympus USA, thanks to the supportive approach of the PR manager, Mr. Kouchi.

1978–80 Received a grant to photograph in Portugal.

1981 Took a trip to Romania. After the amnesty annulling the Czechoslovak conviction of having taken up residence in the Netherlands, without Czechoslovak state permission, was issued a document permitting emigration, and could thus visit the country again.

1982 Visited Poland on the basis of a cultural agreement between Poland and the Netherlands. In collaboration with the Ministry of Culture of the Netherlands, went to Indonesia to document an art-and-education project run by the Dutch painters Pat Andrea and Walter Nobbe at the University of Jakarta and the Bandung Institute of Technology.

1983 Traveled to South America.

1985 The choreographer Jiří Kylián and the director of the Nederlands Dans Theater (NDT), Carl Birnie, made it possible for Dukát to accompany the NDT on their first tour of the Soviet Union. The Cultural Department of the Regional National Committee in Brno refused to grant permission for a Dukát exhibition that had been organized with the curator of the Brno House of Arts, Jana Vránová.

1986 In addition to Portugal, visited Cyprus, Israel, Hungary, and Poland. Borrowed a video camera from Patrick Dadey to explore the potential of the medium.

1987 His photography began to take a back seat to his video recordings.

1988 Won a prize in the documentary-photography category in the Haagse Salon. Invited by Artoteek, The Hague, to take part in an exhibition of six artists in exile who had settled in The Hague in the twentieth century.

1989 At the Gallery of the Association of Czech Photographers, Prague, with the help of Karel Cudlín, installed a three-hour exhibition of small prints brought into the country in the legendary “traveling box” (instead of enlargements). In Czechoslovakia, met with the founders and organizers of FotoFest Houston (USA), Wendy Watriss and Fred Baldwin; recommend by them, received a Leica M6 from Hans-Günther von Zydowitz, the PR manager of Leitz GmbH, West Germany. In the autumn, visited Berlin, and, on 17 November, arrived in Czechoslovakia. During the Velvet Revolution, worked intensively filming demonstrations and other events. (These video recordings have not yet been edited and are still not accessible to the public either in the Czech Republic or abroad.)

1990 After the collapse of the Communist régime in Czechoslovakia, began to visit his home town often. Recorded the post-revolutionary atmosphere in Czechoslovakia, mainly on video.

1991 In the town of Milovice, at one of the main Soviet bases in the country, made video recordings of the withdrawal of the Soviet Army from Czechoslovakia. (The recordings were screened at an exhibition in the Brno House of Arts in 2013, but were not yet widely presented to the Czech public by the mass media.)

1991–94 Went on other trips, either alone or with photographer friends, particularly Karel Cudlín and Jaroslav Pulicar. Their expeditions were in search of people who were not living in the stress caused by the idea that time is money, for example, in Subcarpathian Ruthenia, Poland, and Romania.

1995 The poet Eva Gerlach chose 21 of Dukát's photographs as an inspiration to her collection of verse, *Alles is werkelijk hier* (Everything is really here), with graphic design by Steven van der Gaauw. (The Stedelijk Museum Amsterdam later exhibited it as one of the best-designed books published in the Netherlands in 1997.)

1997 On 26 March, on the occasion of his being awarded the Capi-Lux Alblas Prijs, the most prestigious Dutch prize for a socially important contribution in the arts, a retrospective of Dukát's work opened at the Stedelijk Museum Amsterdam. The awards ceremony speech, entitled "De Osip Mandelsjtam van de fotografie" (The Osip Mandelstam of Photography, a translation of which appears in this volume), was given by Melchior de Wolff.

1998 The Portuguese choreographer Paulo Ribeiro commissioned a video to accompany his ballet, Memórias da pedra – Tempo caido (Memories of stone – Time fallen), which was performed at Expo '98 in Lisbon, and would later be shown in a number of other European and South American cities. An exhibition at the Comenius Museum, Naarden, opened with a speech by Flip Bool, entitled "De doosjes van Vojta Dukát" (The boxes of Vojta Dukát).

2000 During the ceremony at the Letterkundig Museum, The Hague, for the most important Dutch literature prize, the P. C. Hooft Award, won that year by Eva Gerlach, Dukát projected parts of video recordings made in Ukraine. The second edition of their book was published.

2001 Was awarded the Pieter Ouborg Prijs, the arts prize of The Hague. To accompany a retrospective in the Gemeentemuseum, *The Hague, Vojta Dukát / A Slice of Time*, was published, with graphic design by Miroslav Ambroz of Brno, Moravia. It contains not only Dukát's own work, but also important articles about him. Under the aegis of the Stroom Den Haag arts center, he made a video projection called *A Slice of Time*, which was later broadcast by the Kunstkanaal/Arts Channel in the Netherlands.

2002 A video projection was held at BredaPhoto (a photo festival in Breda) and in another nine Dutch towns. For its contribution to humanist art, the book *Vojta Dukát / A Slice of Time* was given an award at the Month of Photography in Bratislava.

2003 At the opening of the new Hague Museum of Photography, Dukát's works were included in the collection of Dutch photography.

2005 On 21 July at 8 p.m., at Quartair, The Hague, 110 years after the brothers Lumière projected the first films, Dukát presented the short video *Tatra 77, Mother of All Cars*, "compilations of video fragments about the aerodynamic Tatra cars, with the aim of indoctrinating the young and the old."

2008 Milan Blatný, at the Institute of Creative Photography, Silesian University, Opava, successfully defended his B.A. thesis, "Vojta Dukát: Fotograf, vynálezce, myslitel"

(V.D.: Photographer, inventor, thinker). In it, he quotes the documentary photographer's credo from T. S. Gottlieb's manuscript, "Obrazy a slova (Záznamy rozhovorů s V. Dukátem)" (Pictures and words: Records of interviews with Dukát): "It is good and very exciting to take the liberty, with humility however, of observing and approaching images at the moment of their genesis, to try and at least a few times during one's lifetime to capture those seemingly perfect ones, those we want to see, those we in fact already know and which occasionally, but to an increasingly lesser degree, do surface from everyday situations."

2009 At the invitation of Bas Vroege, the director of Paradox (a Dutch NGO), Dukát presented the project *Farewell to Arms (Czechoslovakia 1991/2009)* about the withdrawal of the Soviet Army from Czechoslovakia at the Noorderlicht Photofestival, Groningen. Together with Aleš Vašíček, a student at Leiden University, selected part of the video recordings that had been in storage for eighteen years, and digitized them; almost 500 hours of analog recordings, made in various countries, remain, however, unedited.

2011 At the Tina B. Festival of Contemporary Art, Prague, the curator Aleš Vašíček, in the video-art section, presented twenty minutes of unedited video fragments made by Dukát in the town of Milovice, Bohemia, in June 1991, while the Soviet Army was withdrawing from the barracks there.

2012 To mark Dukát's 65th birthday, the Brno House of Arts, 27 years and six months since his exhibition was banned by the Regional National Committee, organized "Photographs from the Box," a retrospective of his work, curated by Jana Vránová.

Životopisná data

1947 12. června narozen v Brně rodičům Emilovi a Marii Dukátovým. Matka je učitelkou, otec vývojovým inženýrem traktorů značky Zetor a fotoamatérem, osobně zpracovávajícím rodinné snímky. Vojta má sestru a bratra.

1953–62 Chodí do školy v Brně na Hroznové ulici, základní vzdělání dokončuje na Křídlovické ulici v Brně.

1962–65 Navštěvuje Střední průmyslovou školu elektrotechnickou v Brně. Mladistvý konstruktér rádií se zpětnou vazbou studium nezavrší, zato si osvojí otcův měchový Voigtländer a promění se v cestovatele a pozorovatele života. Získá fotoaparát značky Ljubitel.

1966 Pracuje jako kulisák v brněnském Mahenově divadle, později Janáčkově opeře v Brně. Po hospitalizaci na psychiatrii na vlastní žádost mu nebylo umožněno vykonávat povinnou vojenskou službu. V léčebně později fotografuje v částečném úvazku experimentální skupinové terapie.

1967–68 Střídá různá zaměstnání a přechází z moravské metropole do české. Opravuje benzínová čerpadla, působí na Akademii výtvarných umění v Praze jako model, pracuje opět jako kulisák, tentokrát v pražském Divadle E. F. Buriana.

1968 Od ledna je osvětlovačem zpravodajství Československé televize, aby získal praxi potřebnou pro pokus o přijetí na obor filmová kamera na FAMU. „Občas mi bylo dovoleno založit film i do kamery Eclair 16 mm," doplňuje při autorizaci svého životopisu v této knize. Zjara si pořídí první kinofilmový fotoaparát. V létě odjíždí na pozvání přátel do Nizozemí. Po okupaci Československa armádami pěti států Varšavské smlouvy zůstává v nizozemském exilu.

1968–70 Studuje fotografii na Akademii Gerrita Rietvelda v Amsterdamu. Z obav, že by prvním ročníkem neprošel, jej pedagog Jaap d'Oliveira přijímá rovnou do třetího semestru na volnou tvorbu.

1969 Získává v Nizozemí status uprchlíka a hojně využívá cestovních dokladů pro osoby bez státní příslušnosti. Několikrát navštěvuje Západní Berlín.

1970–71 Přechází z Akademie Gerrita Rietvelda na Nizozemskou filmovou akademii v Amsterdamu. Studuje kameru, školu však ke konci prvního ročníku opouští.

1972–73 Pobývá často v Římě. Navštěvuje též přátele v Curychu, Paříži a Londýně. Podniká cestu kolem světa, „z finančních důvodů bohužel za méně než osmdesát dní".

1974 V New Yorku se setkává s osmdesátiletým fotografem André Kertészem, který mu zprostředkuje kontakt na Magnum Photos NYC, kde se setkává se Elliottem Erwittem a René Burrim. Stává se nominovaným fotografem agentury Magnum Photos v Paříži, kde udržuje kontakt s Bruno Barbeym.

1975 Spolupracuje na projektu dokumentace města Amsterdamu. Objevuje Portugalsko, kam ho agentura Magnum vyslala, aby fotografoval první volby po karafiátové revoluci. Mimo jiné fotografuje též karnevaly ve Spolkové republice Německo, ve Švýcarsku a soutěže společenských tanců v Nizozemí, Belgii a Velké Británii.

1976 Získává občanství Nizozemského království a grant ministerstva kultury na dokumentaci problematiky odcizení. Stává se podruhé nominovaným fotografem agentury Magnum

Photos. V Maďarsku se po osmi letech setká se svou rodinou. Navštěvuje Jugoslávii a vrací se též do Portugalska.

1977 Jako dokumentarista zaznamenává experimentální terapii narkomanů v Nizozemí. V New Yorku získá fotoaparáty OM 2 od Olympus USA na základě vstřícného postoje PR manažera, pana Kouchiho.

1978–80 Je držitelem grantu pro pobyt v Portugalsku.

1981 Podniká cestu do Rumunska. Po amnestii rozsudku za opuštění ČSSR obdrží doklad o vystěhování, s nímž může navštěvovat ČSSR.

1982 Navštěvuje Polsko na základě kulturní dohody mezi Polskem a Nizozemím. Ve spolupráci s nizozemským ministerstvem kultury dokumentuje v Indonésii umělecko-vzdělávací projekt nizozemských malířů Pata Andrea a Waltera Nobbeho na Univerzitě v Jakartě a Technickém institutu v Bandungu.

1983 Cestuje do Jižní Ameriky.

1985 Choreograf Jiří Kylián a ředitel divadla Carl Birnie umožňují Dukátovi doprovázet Nederlands Dans Theater na prvním turné po Sovětském svazu. Odbor kultury Krajského národního výboru v Brně zamítá Dukátovu výstavu, připravovanou ve spolupráci s kurátorkou Domu umění města Brna, Janou Vránovou.

1986 Vedle Portugalska navštěvuje Kypr, Izrael, Maďarsko a Polsko. Půjčuje si videokameru od Patricka Dadeyho za účelem zkoumání možností tohoto média.

1987 Jeho fotografování začíná ustupovat videozáznamům.

1988 Získává cenu v kategorii dokumentární fotografie při Haagse Salon. Je přizván k výstavě šesti exilových umělců, kteří se ve 20. století usídlili v Haagu (Artoteek, Haag).

1989 V pražské Galerii Svazu českých fotografů instaluje 24. dubna za pomoci Karla Cudlína na tři hodiny malé reprodukce převážené v pověstné cestovní krabičce místo velkých zvětšenin. V Československu se setkává se zakladateli a pořadateli FotoFestu Houston (USA), Wendy Watrissovou a Fredem Baldwinem; na základě jejich doporučení obdrží od pana Hanse-Günthera von Zydowitze, PR manažera Leitz GmbH ve Spolkové republice Německo, fotoaparát Leica M6. Na podzim navštěvuje Berlín a 17. 11. přijíždí do Československa. Během sametové revoluce intenzivně natáčí nejrůznější demonstrace a aktivity. Tyto videomateriály nebyly dosud zpracovány a zpřístupněny širší veřejnosti ani v České republice, ani v zahraničí.

1990 Po skončení moci Komunistické strany Československa navštěvuje častěji své rodné město. Zaznamenává porevoluční nálady a dění v ČSFR, převážně na video.

1991 Videokamerou natáčí stahování okupační armády z Milovic, sídla největší sovětské základny v Československu. Záznamy byly promítány na výstavě v Domě umění v Brně (2013), k jejich zpřístupnění širší veřejnosti v České republice však pro nezájem médií prozatím nedošlo.

1991–94 Podniká další cesty, buď sám či s fotografujícími přáteli, zvláště s Karlem Cudlínem a Jaroslavem Pulicarem. Výpravy směřují za lidmi nestresovanými představou, že čas jsou peníze, například na Podkarpatskou Rus, do Polska a Rumunska.

1995 Básnířka Eva Gerlachová si jako inspiraci vybírá jedenadvacet Dukátových fotografií. Její sbírku Alles is werkelijk hier graficky upravuje Steven van der Gaauw. Stedelijk Museum Amsterdam ji později vystaví jako jednu z publikací vydaných v Nizozemí roku 1997.

1997 Koná se retrospektiva v Stedelijk Museum Amsterdam u příležitosti udělení nejuznávanějšího nizozemského ocenění za umělecký přínos ve fotografii, videu či vizuální sféře Capi-Lux Alblas Prijs (26. března). Laudatio Osip Mandelsjtam van de fotografie pronáší Melchior de Wolff.

1998 Portugalský choreograf Paulo Ribeiro žádá o vytvoření videoprojekce pro baletní představení Memórias da pedra – Tempo caido v rámci kulturních aktivit Světové výstavy Expo '98 v Lisabonu a k prezentacím v řadě dalších evropských a jihoamerických měst. Při zahájení výstavy v Comenius Museu v Naardenu zazní proslov Flipa Boola De doosjes van Vojta Dukát.

2000 V Letterkundig muzeu v Haagu promítá ukázky videozáznamů z Ukrajiny při udílení nejdůležitější nizozemské literární Ceny P. C. Hoofta, kterou toho roku získala Eva Gerlachová. Vychází druhé vydání jejich společné knihy.

2001 Stává se laureátem Pieter Ouborg Prijs, kulturní ceny města Haagu. K retrospektivní výstavě v Gemeentemuseu v Haagu vychází v úpravě Miroslava Ambroze z Brna monografie Vojta Dukát / A Slice of Time. Shrnuje nejen jeho vlastní práce, ale také významné texty o něm. Pod patronací domu umění Stroom Den Haag realizuje videoprojekci A Slice of Time, vysílanou posléze televizním programem Kunstkanaal/Arts Channel.

2002 Koná se videoprojekce na nizozemském festivalu BredaPhoto a v dalších devíti nizozemských městech. Za přínos humanistické tvorbě je na slovenském Měsíci fotografie v Bratislavě vyznamenána monografie Vojta Dukát / A Slice of Time.

2003 Při otevření nového Fotomusea v Haagu je zastoupen na výstavě Fotografie in Nederland.

2005 Quartair v Haagu, 21. 7. ve 20 hodin: 110 let od první projekce bratří Lumièrů promítá krátké video Tatra 77, Mother of All Cars, čili „cílené, indoktrinačně laděné kompilace videofragmentů o aerodynamických vozech Tatra pro staré i mladé".

2008 Milan Blatný obhajuje na Institutu tvůrčí fotografie Slezské univerzity v Opavě životopis Vojta Dukát: Fotograf, vynálezce, myslitel. Dokumentaristovo krédo cituje z rukopisu T. S. Gottlieba Obrazy a slova (Záznamy rozhovorů s V. Dukátem): „Je dobré a velmi vzrušující osmělit se, avšak s pokorou, pozorovat obrazy a přistupovat k nim v okamžiku jejich zrodu, pokusit se alespoň několikrát za život zachytit ty z nich, které jsou zdánlivě dokonalé, ty, které chceme vidět, ty, které ve skutečnosti už známe a které se ve stále menší míře ještě občas vynořují z každodenních situací."

2009 Na pozvání Base Vroegeho, ředitele nizozemské neziskové organizace Paradox, prezentuje projekt Farewell to Arms (Czechoslovakia 1991/2009) o stažení sovětské armády z Československa na Fotofestivalu Noorderlicht v Groningenu. Část osmnáct let odložených videozáznamů digitalizoval v roce 2009, výběr záběrů provedl s Alešem Vašíčkem, toho času studentem Leidenské univerzity. Téměř pět set hodin analogových záznamů z různých zemí zůstává nadále nezpracováno.

2011 Na Festivalu současného umění Praha TINA B. uvádí kurátor Aleš Vašíček v sekci videoartu 20 minut needitovaných videofragmentů, zaznamenaných Vojtou Dukátem v červnu 1991 v Milovicích při odchodu sovětské armády z tamních kasáren.

2012 V roce Dukátových pětašedesátin organizuje kurátorka Jana Vránová v Domě umění města Brna (po dvaceti sedmi a půl letech od zákazu Dukátovy výstavy ze strany KNV) retrospektivu Fotografie z krabičky.

Solo Exhibitions / Samostatné výstavy

1972 Galerie 38, Susan Abelin, Zürich
Galleria Pictogramma, Roma
1973 Galerie 38, Susan Abelin, Zürich
1975 Canon Photo Gallery, Amsterdam
1980 Stedelijk Museum Amsterdam
Galerie Nouvelles Images, Den Haag
Kunstzaal, Hengelo
1989 Galerie Svazu českých fotografů, Praha
1997 Stedelijk Museum Amsterdam
1998 Comenius Museum, Naarden
2001 *A Slice of Time*, Gemeentemuseum, Den Haag
2012 *Photographs from the Box / Fotografie z krabičky*, Dům umění města Brna, Brno

Group Exhibitions / Účast ve skupinových výstavách

1971 On the door of a house in rue Saint-Éleuthère Montmartre, Paris
1971 Roseville Civic Center, Sacramento
1974 Bibliothèque nationale de France, Paris
1976 *Terzijde*, Ministerie van Cultuur, Recreatie en Maatschappelijk Werk, Den Haag
1977 Historisch Museum, Amsterdam
1978 *Dutch Photography after the Second World War / Nederlandse Fotografie na de Tweede Wereldoorlog*, Stedelijk Museum Amsterdam
1983 *Contemporary Dutch Photographers / Hedendaagse Nederlandse Fotografen*, Ministerie van Cultuur, Recreatie en Maatschappelijk Werk, Den Haag, Stedelijk Museum Amsterdam
1984 *7 Dutch Artists*, Elisabeth Frank Gallery, Knokke-le-Zoute
1985 *7 Dutch Photographers / 7 Nederlandse Fotografen, Foto '84*, Nieuwe Kerk, Amsterdam
1985 Cultural Centers in Venlo, Roermond, Maastricht en Heerlen
1985 Museum Fodor / Fotografiemuseum, Amsterdam
1986 *The Animal in Photography, 1840–1986*, The Photographers' Gallery, London
1986 *First Israeli Photography Biennale*, Museum of Art, Ein Harod, Israel
1987 *Photography as an Assignment / Fotografie in opdracht*, Galerie Perspektief, Rotterdam
1988 *Dutch Photography of the 20th Century / Twentieth Century Photography in the Netherlands*, Blaffer Art Museum, PhotoFest, Houston
1988 *Haagsche Nieuwen, 6 buitenlandse kunstenaars of kunstenaars in ballingschap die zich in de 20e eeuw in Den Haag hebben gevestigd*, Artoteek, Den Haag
1989 *Fleeting Images: A Selection from the Work of Twelve Photographers from The Hague / Ogenblikken: Een keuze uit het werk van twaalf Haagse fotografen*, Galerie Nouvelles Images, Den Haag

1989 *Het poëtisch moment*, Stadsgalerij, Heerlen
1989 *150 Years of Photography / 150 Jaar Fotografie*, Stedelijk Museum Amsterdam
1990 *151 Years of Photography / 151 Jaar Fotografie*, Inkt 2, Den Haag
1992 *Czechoslovak Photography in Exile (1939–1989) / Československá fotografie v exilu (1939–1989)*, Výstavní síň S.V.U. Mánes, Praha
1992 *Haagse Kopstukken 1961–1992 / 30 jaar Haagse beeldende kunst in 2 × 28 zelfportretten*, Artoteek, Den Haag
1993 *De Kracht van Heden*, Loods 6, Amsterdam (videofragmenty a videostills na papíře)
1995 Kunst RAI, Amsterdam, Gemeente Museum, Den Haag (videofragmenty prezentované Domeniekem Ruytersem)
1995 Gemeentemuseum, Den Haag (videofragmenty)
1995 *Orbis Fictus. New Media in Contemporary Art / Orbis Fictus. Nová média v současném umění*, Valdštejnská jízdárna, Národní galerie v Praze, Praha (videofragmenty a videostills na papíře)
1998 *Haagsche nieuwen: Den Haag als verblijfplaats en doorgangshuis voor beeldende kunstenaars*, Artoteek, Den Haag
1999 *Dutch Photography Biennale / Nederlandse Fotografie Biennale*, Naarden
1999 *Autonomous Photography in The Hague*, Haagse Kunstkring, Den Haag
2002 *De Kracht van Heden*, Fotofestival, Breda
2002–03 *Fotografen in Nederland*, Fotomuseum, Den Haag
2003 *1000 foto's van Amsterdam 1945–2003*, Historisch Museum, Amsterdam
2003 *Look Light / Ejhle světlo*, Moravská galerie v Brně, Brno
2004 *Le cinéma des photographes Néerlandais*, Maison Européenne de la Photographie, Paris, Institut Néerlandais, Paris (videofragmenty)
2005 Fotofestival, Antwerpen (videofragmenty)
2005 *Nederlands Fotomuseum, Rotterdam* (videofragmenty)
2005 *Czech Photography of the 20th Century / Česká fotografie 20. století*, Galerie hlavního města Prahy, Praha
2007 *Dutch Eyes*, Nederlands Fotomuseum, Rotterdam (videofragmenty)
2007 *Koos Breukel: Nederlandse fotografen*, Nerderlands Fotomuseum, Den Haag
2008 *The Third Side of the Wall. Photography in Czechoslovakia 1969–1988 from the Collection of the Moravian Gallery in Brno / Třetí strana zdi. Fotografie v Československu 1969–1988 ze sbírky Moravské galerie v Brně*, Moravská galerie v Brně, Brno
2008 Gemeentemuseum Den Haag, The XXth Century, Den Haag (videofragmenty)
2009 *Multivocal Histories*, Noorderlicht Photofestival, Groningen (videofragmenty a videostills na papíře)
2011 *Tina B. The Prague Contemporary Art Festival*, Praha (neupravované videofragmenty)

Represented in Collections / Zastoupení ve sbírkách

Artoteek, Den Haag
Gemeente, Amsterdam
Gemeente, Den Haag
Gemeentemuseum, Den Haag
Koninklijke Capi-Lux Alblas Stichting, Amsterdam
Ministerie van Cultuur, Recreatie en Maatschappelijk Werk, Den Haag
Moravská galerie v Brně, Brno
Muzeum Sztuki, Łódź
Nederlandse Kunst Stichting, Amsterdam
Stadsarchief Amsterdam
Stedelijk Museum Amsterdam
Private collections / Soukromé sbírky

Bibliography / Literatura

Books / Knihy

Faye, Jean-Pierre: *Portugal 1974–1975: Regards sur une tentative de pouvoir populaire*, Paris, Hier et demain 1979.

Barents, Els: *Roots & Turns: Traditie en vernieuwing van de fotografie in Nederland vanaf 1900*, Den Haag, SDU 1988.

Balajka, Petr (ed.): *Encyklopedie českých a slovenských fotografů*, Praha, ASCO 1993.

Horová, Anděla (ed.): *Nová encyklopedie českého výtvarného umění*, Praha, Academia 1995.

Dukát, Vojta & Gerlach, Eva: *Alles is werkelijk hier*, Amsterdam, De Arbeiderspers 1997, 2000.

Rudinská, Libuše: *Vojta Dukát – fotografické dílo*, bakalářská práce, Praha, FAMU 1997.

Sena, Antonio: *História da imagem fotográfica em Portugal, 1839–1997*, Oporto, Oporto editora 1998.

Malý, Zbyšek (ed.): *Slovník českých a slovenských výtvarných umělců 1950–1998*, Ostrava, Výtvarné centrum Chagall 1998.

Ginneken, Lily van & Barents, Els & Anema, Taco & Zaal, Louis & Hekking, Veronica, & Drewes, Elsje & Wolff, Melchior de & Bool, Flip & Gerlach, Eva & Dukát, Vojta: *Vojta Dukát / A Slice of Time*, Den Haag, Stroom 2001.

Sinderen van, Wim: *Fotorafen in Nederland. Een anthologie 1852–2002*, Ludion, Fotomuseum Den Haag 2002.

Švácha, Rostislav & Platovská, Marie (ed.): *Dějiny českého výtvarného umění 1958–2000 [VI/2]*, Praha, Academia 2007.

Blatný, Milan: *Vojta Dukát: Fotograf, vynálezce, myslitel*, bakalářská práce, Opava, Slezská univerzita v Opavě 2008.

Gerlach, Eva: *Het gedicht gebeurt nu*, Amsterdam–Antwerpen, De Arbeiderspers 2010.

Vašíček, Aleš: *The role of a curator in the exhibition making process*, supervisor: Prof. Susan Meiselas, Leiden, Universiteit Leiden 2010.
In opdracht, Amsterdam in foto's 1971–75, Amsterdam, Genootschap Amstellodamum, publisher Bas Lubberhuizen 2010.
Birgus, Vladimír & Mlčoch, Jan: *Czech Photography of the 20th Century*, Praha, KANT 2010.
Birgus, Vladimír & Mlčoch, Jan: *Česká fotografie 20. století*, Praha, KANT 2010.
Dufek, Antonín (ed.): *Full Spectrum. Fifty Years of Collecting Photography. The Moravian Gallery in Brno*, Brno & Praha, Moravská galerie v Brně & KANT 2011.
Dufek, Antonín (ed.): *V plném spektru. Fotografie 1841–2005 ze sbírky Moravské galerie v Brně*, Brno & Praha, Moravská galerie v Brně & KANT 2011.

Exhibition Catalogues / Katalogy výstav

Terzijde, Ministerie van Cultuur, Den Haag, Recreatie en Maatschappelijk Werk 1976.
Barents, Els: *Vojta Dukát*, Amsterdam, Stedelijk Museum Amsterdam 1980.
Barents, Els & Kuil, Kees: *7 Dutch Photographers / 7 Nederlandse Fotografen*, Amsterdam, Foto 84 1984.
Barents, Els: *Roots & Turns: Traditie en vernieuwing van de fotografie in Nederland vanaf 1900*, Den Haag, SDU 1988.
Broos, C. H. A. & Santen, Ingrid van & Morel, Michiel: *Haagsche nieuwen: Den Haag als verblijfplaats en doorgangshuis voor beeldende kunstenaars*, Den Haag, Artoteek Den Haag 1988.
Coumans, Willem K. & Laan, Anke van der: *Het poëtisch moment*, Heerlen, Stadsgalerij Heerlen 1989.
Bool, Filip & Kleij, Leo van der & Rijven, Guus: *Fleeting Images: A Selection from the Work of Twelve Photographers from The Hague, Holland / Ogenblikken: Een keuze uit het werk van twaalf Haagse fotografen*, Den Haag, Stichting Hollands Negatief 1989.
Fárová, Anna & Tigrid, Pavel: *Czechoslovak Photography in Exile (1939–1989) / Československá fotografie v exilu (1939–1989)*, Praha, Asociace fotografů 1992.
Santen, Ingrid van & Welling, Dolf: *Haagse Kopstukken 1961–1992 / 30 jaar Haagse beeldende kunst in 2 × 28 zelfportretten*, Den Haag, Artotheek Den Haag 1992.
Andriesse, Paul (ed.): *De Kracht van Heden*, Amsterdam, Loods 6 1993.
Smolíková, Marta (ed.): *Orbis Fictus. New Media in Contemporary Art / Orbis Fictus. Nová média v současném umění*, Praha, Oswald 1995.
Sei, Keiko (ed.): *Orbis Fictus. New Media in Contemporary Art / Orbis Fictus. Nová média v současném umění*, Praha, Oswald 1995.
Zemánek, Jiří (ed.): *Look Light / Ejhle světlo*, Brno, Moravská galerie v Brně 2003.
Birgus, Vladimír & Mlčoch, Jan: *Czech Photography of the 20th Century. A Guide*, Praha, Uměleckoprůmyslové museum v Praze & KANT 2005.
Birgus, Vladimír & Mlčoch, Jan: *Česká fotografie 20. století / Průvodce*, Praha, Uměleckoprůmyslové museum v Praze & KANT 2005.
Bool, Flip & Boom, Mattie & Gierstberg, Frits (ed.): *Dutch Eyes. A Critical History of Photography in the Netherlands*, Rotterdam, Nederlands Fotomuseum 2007.
Dufek, Antonín: *The Third Side of the Wall. Photography in Czechoslovakia 1969–1988 from the*

Collection of the Moravian Gallery in Brno / Třetí strana zdi. Fotografie v Československu 1969–1988 ze sbírky Moravské galerie v Brně, Brno & Praha, Moravská galerie v Brně & KANT 2008.
Bas, Vroege: *Multivocal Histories*, Noorderlicht Photofestival, Groningen, 2009.
Dvořáková, Valerie & Polifková, Petra (ed.): *TINA B. The Prague Contemporary Art Festival*, Praha, Galerie Vernon 2011.
Vránová, Jana: *Vojta Dukát*, Brno, Dům umění města Brna 2012.

Video

Vojta Dukát / A Slice of Time, Stroom Haags centrum voor beeldende kunst & Amsterdams Fonds voor de Kunst & Kunstkanaal/Art Channel, 2001.
Vojta Dukát / A Slice of Time, Paris, Maison Européenne de la Photographie, 2004.
Interview VPRO, De Plantage, Hanneke Groenteman, 1998 (TV).

Articles / Články

Gasser, Manuel (ed.): *DU, Kulturelle Monatsschrift*, portfolio, 1973, č. 2, Zürich.
Bardawil, Georges (ed.): *Le nouveau Photo Cinéma*, portfolio, 1976, č. 9, Le Chêne, Paris.
Maye, Patricia (ed.): *Nikon World*, portfolio, 1978, č. 10, Nikon Inc., USA.
Barents, Els: Poëtische fotojournalistiek van Vojta Dukát, *Bijvoorbeeld – Vormgeving en Kunst*, 14, 1982, č. 2.
Anema, Taco & Zaal, Louis: Ik heb geen behoefte om "het kwaad" uit te drukken, *De Groene Amsterdammer*, 6 juni 1984, s. 20.
Balajka, Petr: Jednodenní výstava v Galerii SČF, *Československá fotografie* 40, 1989, č. 9, s. 402–403.
Algera, Kirsten & Broek, Martijn van den: De Kracht van Heden, *Vormgeving en Bouwkunst*, 1993.
Hekking, Veronica: Portfolio De foto's van Vojta Dukát. Licht en beweging genoteerd, *Hollands Licht* 2, 2e kwartaal 1997.
Marsman, Eddie: Op foto's Vojta Dukát doet niemand iets vervelends, NRC, 1997, č. 4.
Blom, Onno: Poëzie in andere verpakking, *Kunst*, December 1997.
Divendal, Leo: Uit de diepte van Europa, *Foto*, 1997, č. 5.
Marsman, Eddie: Fotograaf Dukát heeft aan weinig genoeg, NRC, 2001.
Professional Photography, portfolio, Netherland, 2002.
Dufek, Antonín: A Slice of Time by Vojta Dukát, *Imago*, 2002, č. 14, s. 67–68.
Ollier, Brigitte: Plans de Bataves. Le regard des photographes néerlandais sur le monde, de 1917 à 2002, à travers 60 films projetés à Paris, *Liberation*, Paris, 24. 4. 2004.

List of Published Photographs

36 Cochabamba, Bolivia, 1983
37 Kalwaria Zebrzydowska, Poland, 1986
38 Portugal, *sine anno*
39 Cracow, Poland, 1986
40 Humahuaca, Argentina, 1983
41 Colonia del Sacramento, Uruguay, 1983
42 Leiria, Portugal, 1975
43 Łódź, Poland, 1988
44 Humahuaca, Argentina, 1983
45 Viana do Castelo, Portugal, 1977
46 Blackpool, Great Britain, 1978
47 Cracow, Poland, 1986
48 Java, Indonesia, 1982
49 Cracow, Poland, 1982
50 Kalwaria Zebrzydowska, Poland, 1984
51 Fiji, 1973
52 Potosí, Bolivia, 1983
53 Portugal, *sine anno*
54 Kalwaria Zebrzydowska, Poland, 1986
55 Porto, Portugal, 1978
56 Cracow, Poland, 1982
57 Viana do Castelo, Portugal, 1975
58 Spoleto, Italy, 1974
59 Castel Gandolfo, Italy, 1972
60 Kalwaria Zebrzydowska, Poland, 1986
61 Berlin, Germany, 1973
62 American Samoa, 1973
63 Rome, Italy, 1974
64 Porto, Portugal, 1977
65 Rome, Italy, 1972
66 Mondim de Basto, Portugal, 1977
67 Ponte de Lima, Portugal, 1976
68 Nazaré, Portugal, 1978
69 Near La Paz, Bolivia, 1983
70 Clingendael, The Hague, the Netherlands, 1974
71 Western Samoa, 1973
72 Suva, Fiji, 1973
73 Zurich, Switzerland, 1979
74 Humahuaca, Argentina, 1983
75 Oruro, Bolivia, 1983
76 Spoleto, Italy, 1974
77 Near Vizovice, Moravia, 1988
78 Vatican City, 1974

Seznam publikovaných fotografií

s. 2 foto: Vojta Dukát
s. 18 foto: Vojta Dukát, 1977
s. 26 foto: Miroslav Ambroz
s. 40 foto: Miloš Stejskal, 1976
s. 48 foto: Kastermans / Dukát, 1998
1 Kalwaria Zebrzydowska, Polsko, 1986
2 Kalwaria Zebrzydowska, Polsko, 1982
3 Mourão, Portugalsko, 1975
4 Lisabon, Portugalsko, 1975
5 Viana do Castelo, Portugalsko, 1976
6 Burgos, Španělsko, 1975
7 Kalwaria Zebrzydowska, Polsko, 1982
8 Viana do Castelo, Portugalsko, 1976
9 São Bartolomeu-do-Mar, Esposende, Portugalsko, 1977
10 Fátima, Portugalsko, 1978
11 Nossa Senhora da Mó, Portugalsko, 1979
12 Ostrovy Fidži, 1973
13 Vídeň, Rakousko, 1977
14 Viana do Castelo, Portugalsko, 1977
15 Beja, Portugalsko, 1975
16 Leningrad, Sovětský svaz, 1985
17 Copacabana, Jezero Titicaca, Bolívie, 1983
18 Lisabon, Portugalsko, 1979
19 Řím, Itálie, 1972
20 Kalwaria Zebrzydowska, Polsko, 1986
21 Západní Samoa, 1973
22 Kalifornie, USA, 1973
23 Curych, Švýcarsko, 1979
24 Częstochowa, Polsko, 1986
25 Vilar-Formoso, Portugalsko, 1975
26 Basilej, Švýcarsko, 1979
27 Řím, Itálie, 1972
28 Łódź, Polsko, 1988
29 Kalwaria Zebrzydowska, Polsko, 1982
30 Portugalsko, 1977
31 Portugalsko, 1976
32 Poblíž La Pazu, Bolívie, 1983
33 Jeruzalém, Izrael, 1986
34 Porto, Portugalsko, 1977
35 Coroico, Bolívie, 1983

36 Cochabamba, Bolívie, 1983
37 Kalwaria Zebrzydowska, Polsko, 1986
38 Portugalsko, bez data
39 Krakov, Polsko, 1986
40 Humahuaca, Argentina, 1983
41 Colonia del Sacramento, Uruguay, 1983
42 Leiria, Portugalsko, 1975
43 Łódź, Polsko, 1988
44 Humahuaca, Argentina, 1983
45 Viana do Castelo, Portugalsko, 1977
46 Blackpool, Velká Británie, 1978
47 Krakov, Polsko, 1986
48 Java, Indonésie, 1982
49 Krakov, Polsko, 1982
50 Kalwaria Zebrzydowska, Polsko, 1984
51 Ostrovy Fidži, 1973
52 Potosí, Bolívie, 1983
53 Portugalsko, bez data
54 Kalwaria Zebrzydowska, Polsko, 1986
55 Porto, Portugalsko, 1978
56 Krakov, Polsko, 1982
57 Viana do Castelo, Portugalsko, 1975
58 Spoleto, Itálie, 1974
59 Castel Gandolfo, Itálie, 1972
60 Kalwaria Zebrzydowska, Polsko, 1986
61 Berlín, Německo, 1973
62 Americká Samoa, 1973
63 Řím, Itálie, 1974
64 Porto, Portugalsko, 1977
65 Řím, Itálie, 1972
66 Mondim de Basto, Portugalsko, 1977
67 Ponte de Lima, Portugalsko, 1976
68 Nazaré, Portugalsko, 1978
69 Poblíž La Pazu, Bolívie, 1983
70 Clingendael, Den Haag, Nizozemí, 1974
71 Západní Samoa, 1973
72 Suva, Ostrovy Fidži, 1973
73 Curych, Švýcarsko, 1979
74 Humahuaca, Argentina, 1983
75 Oruro, Bolívie, 1983
76 Spoleto, Itálie, 1974
77 Poblíž Vizovic, Morava, 1988
78 Vatikán, 1974

Vojta Dukát

Essays by Antonín Dufek, Melchior de Wolff, Vojta Dukát
Photograph selection: Miroslav Ambroz & Vojta Dukát
Biography and bibliography: Miroslav Ambroz & Milan Blatný & Josef Moucha
Translation: essay by Antonín Dufek – Derek & Marzia Paton,
essay by Melchior de Wolff – Miloš Stejskal & Tony Long,
essays by Vojta Dukát – Vojta Dukát, essay by Vojta Dukát / T. S. Gottlieb –
Vojta Dukát & J. E. Keats
Graphic concept: Studio Najbrt, Prague
Graphic design: Aleš Najbrt & Martina Krýslová, Studio Najbrt
Prepress: Marvil, Prague & Miroslav Ambroz
Printed by PB tisk, Příbram
Copy editors: Jan Šulc & Derek Paton
Published by TORST
Address: Opatovická 24, Prague 1
CZ-110 00, Czech Republic
foto@torst.cz
First edition, 2013

Also available through D. A. P. / Distributed Art Publishers
155 Sixth Avenue, 2nd Floor, New York, N.Y. 10013, USA
Tel: ++1 (212) 627–1999 Fax: ++1 (212) 627–9484